A Handbook for

Citizens Living Abroad

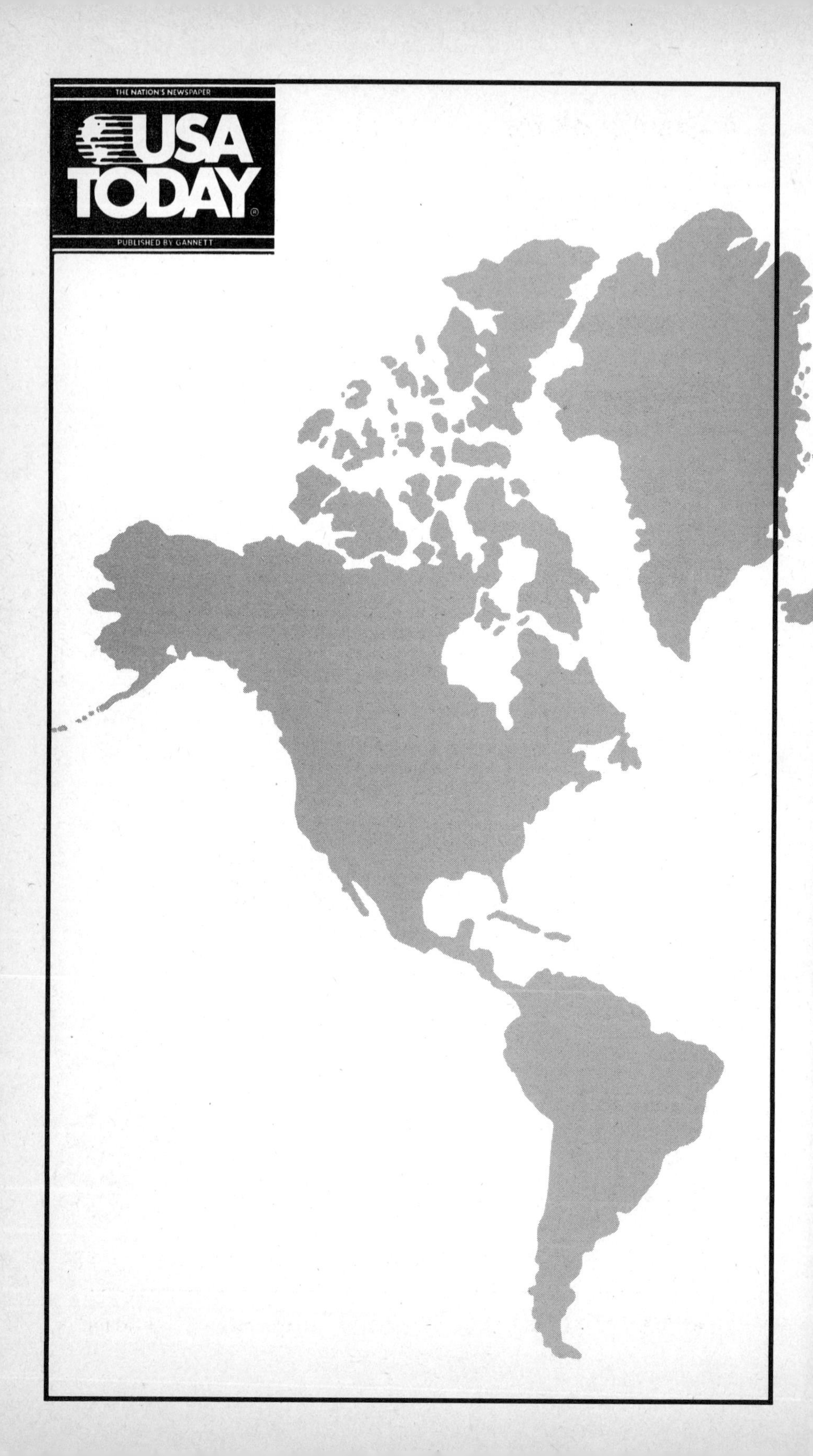
THE NATION'S NEWSPAPER
USA TODAY
PUBLISHED BY GANNETT

A Handbook for

Citizens Living Abroad

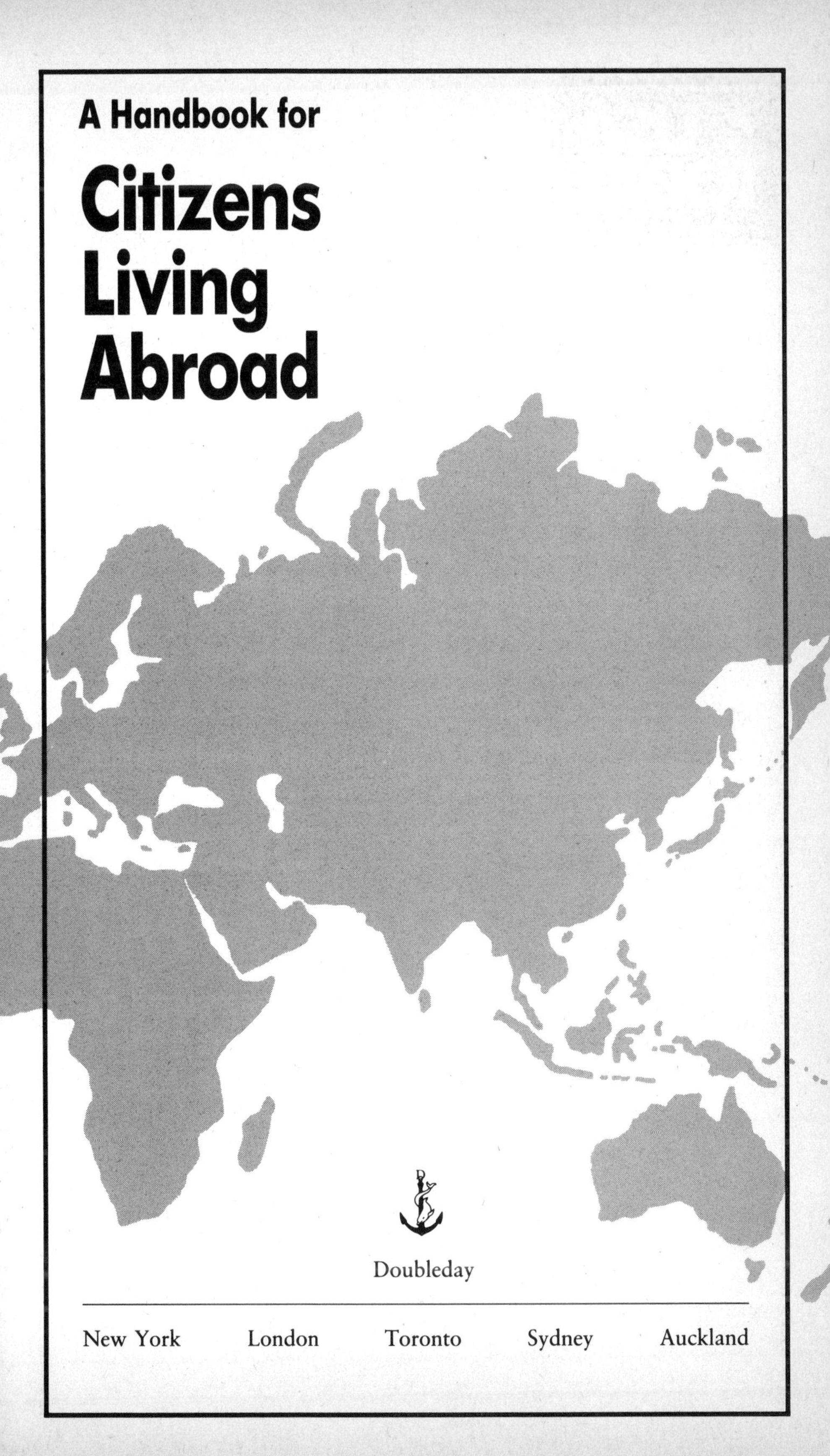

Doubleday

New York London Toronto Sydney Auckland

PUBLISHED BY DOUBLEDAY
a division of Bantam Doubleday Dell Publishing Group, Inc.
666 Fifth Avenue, New York, New York 10103

DOUBLEDAY and the portrayal of an anchor
with a dolphin are trademarks of Doubleday,
a division of Bantam Doubleday Dell Publishing
Group, Inc.

First published in 1988, in slightly different form, by USA TODAY Books under the title *USA Citizens Abroad: A Handbook.*

Library of Congress Cataloging-in-Publication Data
A handbook for citizens living abroad / by American Citizens
Abroad.
p. cm.
Rev. ed. of: USA citizens abroad. 1988.
1. Americans—Legal status, laws, etc.—Foreign countries.
2. Emigration and immigration law—United States. 3. Americans—Handbooks, manuals, etc. 4. American Citizens Abroad (Organization) 5. USA citizens abroad. I. Title: Handbook for U.S. citizens abroad. II. Title: Handbook for US citizens abroad. III. Title: USA Today's handbook for US citizens abroad.
KF390.A5U83 1990
342.73'082—dc20
[347.30282] 89-25962
CIP

BOOK DESIGN BY STEPHEN S. QUINE DESIGN

ISBN 0-385-26590-5

PRINTED IN THE UNITED STATES OF AMERICA
JUNE 1990
BG

Foreword

This handbook was prepared by American Citizens Abroad (ACA)—a private, non-profit, educational organization that is not affiliated with any political party or other partisan organization in the USA or abroad.

Comments and suggestions are welcome. Letters should be sent to:

- The Editors
  ACA Handbook
  157 Route du Grand Lancy
  1213 Onex, Geneva
  Switzerland

American Citizens Abroad feels a responsibility to remind U.S. citizens abroad that, while U.S. government officials are stationed abroad to serve them, these officials also have a responsibility to enforce laws and regulations.

In carrying out their duties, U.S. government officials at embassies and consulates frequently are required to file reports of conversations they have had with U.S. citizens concerning any number of different matters. U.S. citizens should be cautious about making unreflective or flippant statements to U.S. government officials. Such statements could be used against them.

In case of doubt about what to say or how to respond to requests for information from the U.S. government, U.S. citizens abroad should first consider consulting a lawyer or other competent counsel.

This handbook is not a legal document or manual.

Information in this handbook on U.S. laws, regulations, and policies is intended only as a general guide. Because specific details make every situation unique, citizens are encouraged to consult the appropriate U.S. government agency for definitive information.

While every effort has been made to obtain and provide accurate and current information, American Citizens Abroad, USA TODAY, Gannett Co. Inc., and Doubleday decline all responsibility for any problems or losses that might arise from the use of this information.

Readers who have specific problems relating to any areas addressed in this handbook are strongly advised to consult the appropriate U.S. government authorities and to seek advice from qualified lawyers and/or accountants.

Preface

Many U.S. citizens have mixed and conflicting emotions about fellow citizens who live abroad. Their pride in U.S. institutions and the U.S. way of life often generates resentment toward anyone who voluntarily leaves the USA. They can be suspicious that U.S. citizens going abroad might have ulterior motives.

There is often a certain envy among the home folks of the opportunities U.S. citizens abroad have to broaden their horizons, and they often incorrectly assume that these citizens are living lives of luxury in exotic places.

What escapes the notice of many U.S. citizens living in the USA is that those abroad have most of the same responsibilities and obligations without (some argue) the usual rights, privileges, and benefits that those at home might take for granted.

U.S. citizens abroad bear the unfamiliar burden of being aliens in foreign societies. Sometimes the financial rewards, as generous as they might seem, are insufficient compensation for intangible and psychological burdens. Frequently, the financial reward is illusory because of the cost of living in the foreign land.

The USA needs citizens who are willing to become U.S. citizens abroad. We need military personnel willing to serve abroad to protect our allies and stand as a first line of defense of our country. Military families constitute almost one-fourth of our population abroad.

We need Foreign Service personnel who, along with their families, go abroad to represent and promote U.S. interests and to provide needed services and assistance to private U.S. citizens.

We need business executives, sales representatives, technicians, lawyers, and accountants to sell and service U.S. products abroad. These U.S. citizens abroad help create jobs to produce those products at home and, by increasing export revenues, help us pay for products we want to import.

We need teachers, scholars, scientists, students, and artists to extend an appreciation of U.S. culture to others and to bring back what they have learned to enrich our own culture.

The mixed emotions about U.S. citizens abroad have resulted in some unique rules and regulations governing relations between individuals and their homeland. Some of these rules are just complex, but some literally defy understanding by those to whom they are directed. Some are well known, while others are obscure.

In dealing with various topics, we follow a modified question and answer format. We begin each chapter by noting fundamental principles on which the rules and regulations are based. The questions and answers illustrate the most common cases that arise and how they might be resolved. Some unusual cases are also included.

Acknowledgments

Many individuals and organizations have helped ACA prepare this handbook. ACA wishes to acknowledge the particular helpfulness of the Bureau of Consular Affairs of the Department of State, the Federal Voting Assistance Program Office of the Department of Defense, and the Social Security Administration.

Andy Sundberg, one of the founders of ACA, suggested the idea for the handbook and has been the driving force in seeing it through to publication. Bill Yoffee, who formerly worked for the Social Security Administration and for ACA in Washington, was a major contributor to the handbook, as was Tom Johnson, a U.S. lawyer living in London, who wrote the chapter on taxation. Ruth Sundberg proofread the original manuscript.

Also instrumental in creating this handbook were: Ursula Shears, Martha Hartman, Bob Angarola, Roberta Enschede, Lisa Farrell, Dorothy Oliveau, and ACA Director John Iglehart.

Phyllis Michaux, a consultant for ACA, assisted in research and editing.

Contributors from Gannett News Service: J. Ford Huffman, managing editor/features, graphics and photography; Theresa Klisz Harrah, assistant news editor/features; Randy Kirk, USA TODAY Books editor; and Elizabeth Allen Goodrich, news assistant.

And from Gannett New Media: Nancy Woodhull, president; Phil Fuhrer, vice president; and Emilie Davis, managing editor.

Finally, ACA is most grateful to David Mazzarella, president of Gannett International, which publishes the International Edition of USA TODAY, whose wisdom and commercial acumen made possible the publication of this handbook.

Contents

Chapter 1

Who's Living Abroad

Introduction

When you leave the USA to live in a foreign country, you will join an estimated 2.5 million to 3 million other U.S. citizens living outside the country (excluding military personnel but including their dependents).

- One-quarter live in Canada.
- One-quarter live in Western Europe.
- About 9% live in Mexico.

The rest live in 100 other foreign countries.

Some of these U.S. citizens are permanent residents of one country. Others reside outside of the USA for long periods of time, moving from country to country.

U.S. communities abroad vary greatly in size from one country to another. For example, there are fewer than 100 U.S.

citizens living in Mauritius and more than 300,000 living in West Germany.

U.S. business professionals are stationed abroad on temporary and permanent assignments and are employed by large international corporations as well as by smaller companies.

Others are self-employed.

Some are U.S. journalists covering news abroad.

Also abroad:

Members of U.S. delegations to international organizations such as UNESCO, the International Labor Organization, the World Bank and International Monetary Fund, the European Economic Community, the World Health Organization, and the International Atomic Energy Agency. Some U.S. citizens are permanent staff members of these organizations.

Officials of federal agencies, including the State, Treasury, Labor, Defense and Justice departments.

Personnel from the U.S. Information Agency. They organize conferences and distribute books and other materials about the USA to citizens of your host country.

Representatives of the Internal Revenue Service. They can help you fill out your tax form.

Representatives of the Commercial Section, staffed by the Department of Commerce. They will help with your business needs.

State trade offices. Most states maintain offices abroad to promote their local exports and encourage foreign investments to create new jobs in the USA. The addresses of these state trade offices can be obtained from either the Commercial Offices of the U.S. Embassy nearest you, or from an American Chamber of Commerce abroad.

Retirees. Social Security payments are made to more than 200,000 U.S. citizens residing in more than 100 countries. Most retirees are in Mexico, Canada, Italy, and West Germany.

In addition:

More than 650 U.S. colleges and universities have study

programs abroad. Between 25,000 and 30,000 students are in these programs.

Many U.S. citizens abroad teach English in foreign schools at the secondary and graduate levels, as well as in language schools for adults.

Organizations Abroad

There are many U.S. organizations of a benevolent or social nature abroad. Some are outposts of U.S.-based groups; others have been established within the communities.

More than 500 private U.S. voluntary organizations conduct relief and development operations abroad. Information about them can be obtained from:

- Interaction/American Council
  for Voluntary International Action
  1815 H St. N.W.
  11th floor
  Washington, DC 20006

American women's clubs and American men's clubs are found around the world, especially in the major world cities.

Many of the women's clubs are affiliated with the Federation of American Women's Clubs Overseas (FAWCO), and many of the men's clubs are affiliated with the Federation of International American Clubs (FIAC).

There are also a number of U.S. men's and women's clubs that are not part of these organizations. The locations of women's and men's clubs can be obtained from your nearest U.S. embassy or consulate, and also from local U.S. churches and schools.

The U.S. Democratic and Republican parties are active abroad.

These organizations are called Democrats Abroad and Republicans Abroad. Both parties allow U.S. citizens abroad to send delegates to their national committee meetings and also to their presidential conventions. Your local U.S. embassy or consulate should have a list of these organizations and information on how to contact them.

Two organizations have been very active and successful in proposing changes to U.S. laws and regulations that affect overseas citizens: American Citizens Abroad (ACA) in Geneva, Switzerland, and the Association of American Residents Overseas (AARO) in Paris, France.

The Veterans of Foreign Wars has posts in France, West Germany, Panama, Taiwan, and Thailand. There are American Legion posts in Canada, West Germany, England, France, Ireland, Italy, Mexico, Panama, Costa Rica, Thailand, Japan, and the Philippines.

The Daughters of the American Revolution has chapters in England, France, Canada, and Mexico.

Two organizations in Paris serve the visually handicapped. The English Language Library for the Blind distributes "talking books" on cassette tapes to blind persons in France and other European countries. The French branch of the Hadley School for the Blind offers correspondence courses in English to blind students.

And there are many more. Ask at your consulate which U.S. groups are located in your destination city. Unless it is in the most remote spot, you will not have to worry about getting homesick.

Chapter 2

Moving and Settling Abroad

Introduction

Nearly everyone who goes abroad for any reason needs a passport. Brief trips by U.S. citizens to Canada and Mexico are the primary exceptions, but even in those cases you will need something to identify you as a U.S. citizen. More importantly, you will need that identification to show U.S. border authorities when you return.

If you are leaving the North American continent or returning to the USA from abroad, the transportation company will ask to see your passport. If the company accepts you as a passenger without a passport and you are turned away at your destination, the company must pay the cost of taking you back and might be fined.

Passports and Visas

What is a passport and what is its real significance for me as a traveler?

A passport is an identity document that is issued by virtually every country to its citizens. However, the fact that every country issues them does not mean that every country gives the same recognition to the holders of other countries' passports.

If you read your U.S. passport, you will see that it identifies you as a citizen/national of the USA and that the secretary of state requests others to permit you "to pass without delay or hindrance and in case of need to give all lawful aid and protection." Whether or not this request is honored depends upon a number of things, including relations between the USA and the other country and your personal background and conduct. There are no guarantees.

Your best guarantee of passport recognition is to be assured before you leave the USA that you will be received hospitably at your destination. While there, behave like the guest you are.

Most foreigners, particularly Europeans, take their passports very seriously. Some have routine difficulty proving their citizenship when they cross international boundaries. The value of a passport to you while you are abroad cannot be overemphasized.

How do I obtain a passport?

File a one-page application form at your nearest passport office. Forms are also available at many post offices with instructions on where to file. You will need a birth certificate or other evidence of citizenship and two passport-size photos. If you are obtaining a passport for the first time, the fee is $42 for persons age 18 and older, $27 for minors. You must file in person. The passport is valid for 10 years.

If you are renewing a passport that has been issued within the past 12 years, the fee is $35 for persons age 18 and older and $20 for minors.

Can passports be issued abroad?

Yes. U.S. consulates and embassies abroad can issue new passports and renew existing ones (see Chapter 7, "Consular Services Abroad").

Are there different types of passports?

Yes. The USA issues three types: Regular (blue cover); Official (maroon cover); and Diplomatic (black cover).

Regular passports are issued to all U.S. citizens who request and pay for them.

Official passports are issued without charge to U.S. government civilian personnel who go abroad on official assignments and to their accompanying family members.

Diplomatic passports are issued without charge to accredited diplomats and to some VIPs and their accompanying family members.

Military personnel going abroad to serve with military units ordinarily do not carry passports because their military IDs serve the same purpose. But they might need passports for certain kinds of travel while they are abroad. Normally, their accompanying family members obtain regular passports.

Must my spouse and children each have a passport?

Yes. It is no longer possible to have a single passport issued for several family members.

How do I protect my passport?

Don't carry your passport with you if you are staying in one place for a while. Put it in a safe place where it will be available if you need it.

When you are traveling, keep it on your person—in a zippered pocket if possible. Unsafe places: a backpack, suitcase, handbag, or briefcase.

If you are stopping over in a place that has facilities for storing valuables, you might want to leave your passport there.

If the hotel keeper asks for your passport to show the local police, ask for a receipt. It is not a good idea to entrust your passport to anyone about whom you have any doubts. If someone wants to hold your passport as security for anything, make other arrangements.

Don't lend your passport to anyone.

Keep several extra passport photos handy with a record of your passport number and the date and place of issue. You might also want to make a photocopy to keep separately. An out-of-date (canceled) passport can be useful when applying for a new one as it might expedite paperwork.

What should I do if I lose my passport?

Report it immediately to the nearest U.S. consulate or embassy.

What are the main uses for my passport?

You will use your passport when crossing international boundaries, conducting financial transactions such as converting dollars to local currency, or when identifying yourself to local police or public officials. If you need help from a U.S. consulate or embassy, you will also need to show your passport.

What is a visa, and how does it differ from a passport?

A visa is the host country's permission for you to travel or stay there. It is usually stamped in a valid passport. U.S. tourists and temporary visitors no longer need them in many countries. Some countries issue them at the border when you arrive, but others require them to be issued before you arrive, especially if your stay is likely to be a long one.

It is best to check with the nearest consulate of the country you intend to visit. Travel agents can be helpful, but they do not always have the most up-to-date information.

Be precise about your reasons for going and how long you intend to stay. If you have a special type of passport (official or diplomatic), be sure to mention it. Reason: A few countries still consider it a courtesy to enter a visa in these special passports, even though they do not do so for regular passports.

It might take awhile to obtain a visa, so start early. The foreign consulate issuing the visa might also impose a fee.

If the country you intend to visit does not have a consulate near you, try writing to its embassy in Washington, D.C., or consult the Washington, D.C., phone directory or the State Department diplomatic list in your local library.

Remember: Living in a foreign country as a foreigner might require some special formalities when leaving and re-entering that country. Before you leave, make sure you have the correct visa or other documentation to permit you to re-enter.

A member of my family who will accompany me abroad is a resident alien, not a U.S. citizen. What precautions must we take to assure no loss of status?

The person involved could be in one of three categories: a foreign citizen, a refugee, or a stateless person.

The foreign citizen should have a valid passport from his or her country.

The refugee or stateless person without a valid passport might need a *laissez-passer*. This is merely an identity document and accords no rights of citizenship.

If the member of the family who is a resident alien has been admitted to the USA for permanent residence (a "green-card holder"), then that family member is entitled to leave and return. Such a person should check with the Immigration and Naturalization Service of the Department of Justice before leaving the USA to be sure that all papers are in order.

Leaving the USA could delay qualifying for U.S. citizenship, and there are many conditions that could require starting that process all over. There are also some special situations that arise under U.S. Social Security laws and income tax laws for resident aliens abroad.

Health Preparations

Are any special health preparations and precautions necessary for living abroad?

It depends on where you will be living and traveling. In most industrialized countries, no special precautions are necessary. But in the developing world, whether required or not, it is advisable to obtain a range of immunizations or booster shots. Your personal physician is the best source of advice.

Many countries require AIDS tests for non-citizens planning to work or live in the countries for a long period of time. Information on those requirements, immunizations needed, and other health recommendations can be obtained from:

- U.S. Public Health Service
  Centers for Disease Control
  Atlanta, GA 30333

What about my personal health needs?

A thorough physical examination before you go abroad to live is recommended. Many employers require this.

Take copies of your dental charts if you have had extensive dental work that might need treatment.

If you have had any special medical problems, ask your physician for a "Medical Passport," which will list the problems and recommended treatments if they recur. Ask your pharmacist for the generic names of your prescription drugs. This enables pharmacies abroad to match them with local equivalents.

What about private health insurance?

Make adequate arrangements before you go. You might find it more difficult and more expensive to buy private health insurance abroad than in the USA. It is unlikely you will qualify immediately for care under the host country's national medical care or insurance plan, if there is one. At the outset, you are on your own.

You might already have the insurance you need through your private policy or through your employer's plan. Check. If not, you might be able to purchase a rider to your existing policy.

Medicare is not available to U.S. citizens abroad. If any elderly persons come to visit you while you are living abroad, advise them to take out private coverage.

You should be prepared to pay for medical care out of pocket when you first go abroad. Most policies available in the USA will reimburse you for part or all of your allowable expenses after you have paid them and submitted a claim with receipts. There could be considerable delays.

You might want to make financial arrangements with a local physician or hospital before any illness occurs.

Packing and Moving

Is moving abroad very different from moving within the USA?

Getting estimates, discussing packing materials, and selecting a mover are much the same as when you move at home. Most large moving companies will handle international shipments either on their own or in cooperation with one or more other firms at points of transfer and destination.

Should I insure against loss or damage?

Yes. Your household effects will be moved by road to a seaport, transferred to a ship, transferred again for further road or rail shipment, and finally delivered either to your new home or to a storage warehouse. They will remain in the warehouse until you find housing. The risk of loss or damage will be much greater than it is for a domestic move, so you must insure accordingly. Consider whether you want to insure for actual cash value or replacement value.

What can I do to protect my belongings against loss or damage?

Try to keep the number of firms involved to a minimum to avoid confusion about responsibility. Select the fewest number of transfers to minimize opportunities for damage and loss.

If your belongings must go into storage at the other end, it might help to have them packed in lift vans, which are nailed shut when they leave your U.S. home and need not be opened again until they are delivered to you. Containerized shipments are safe but entail loose storage and increase the danger of theft at the receiving end.

How long will the shipment take?

This depends on your destination. It might be anywhere from two weeks to two or more months. If you will need more than you can take with you, consider sending a few things via air freight—you will have them before your main shipment arrives.

Should I take the entire contents of my household?

Unlike moving in the USA, moving abroad means leaving behind your plants, foodstuffs (unless tightly sealed), and liquor, unless you are prepared to pay customs duty (see Chapter 9, "Customs Requirements"). You should take your electrical appliances only if the voltage is appropriate for your destination or if you have transformers to adapt them. Beyond that, some knowledge of the climate and type of housing (it could be furnished) at your destination is essential to help you decide what to take, what to leave in storage, and what to buy before you go.

Where can I get this information?

Your employer and your predecessor might help. The State Department provides its officers and staff with a report on the country and city to which they are being assigned. More specific information is contained in local guidebooks published by and for U.S. communities abroad.

These guidebooks generally deal with climate and clothing,

schools and housing, shopping, leisure, and other details of daily living. They usually include what you need to know about local laws, such as how to obtain residence and work permits, pay taxes, and register your car, dog, TV and radio sets.

Where can I get such a guidebook?

American women's clubs abroad are the usual source, but other U.S. organizations, including American Chambers of Commerce abroad, might help you establish contact.

Driving Abroad

What about a driver's license?

In many countries, you are allowed to use your U.S. license for a limited time. But it is wiser to obtain an International Driver's License before you leave the USA. This is available for a small fee from your AAA club. You will need a recent passport-size photo for the license.

Once you are settled and have registered your car, you might find that you must acquire a local driver's license. You might have to take a written examination and, in some cases, a driving test. Obtain a local driver's manual if one is available.

What about auto insurance?

Auto liability insurance is essential when owning and driving a car abroad. Most countries require it and will not allow the car on the road if you can't provide proof of insurance.

Your home policy ordinarily will not suffice. Your U.S. insurer or agent might be able to provide a policy rider for you while you are abroad, but if you expect to be there for an extended time you should check into the policies available.

The following forms of insurance coverage for driving abroad are not required but are advisable:

Legal protection insurance to cover legal defense, and bail-bond insurance to cover possible situations where the alternative is jail while awaiting trial. This is not common, but it could happen.

Comprehensive and collision insurance (with deductible) are advisable. Special short-term coverage is available for trips to third countries—a good idea when visiting countries in which liability insurance is not mandatory.

Should I take my automobile?

If you have to pay to ship it, you might find it is cheaper to buy a car while you are abroad. Also: In some countries you might find that foreigners who import a car have to pay a tax that offsets the price of buying a new car locally. If you work for an employer who requires you to have a car, your employer might offer some advice or financial assistance.

Remember that having a U.S.-made car (especially a large one) abroad can be very expensive in fuel and maintenance charges and might require costly adjustments to meet local specifications.

Banking and Credit

When you arrive at your destination, you will have an immediate need for money. Coping with short-term cash problems is relatively easy if you have major credit cards, traveler's checks, and local currency. Long-term arrangements need advance preparation.

Your banking and credit arrangements abroad will be easier if you have a solid banking relationship in the USA before you start.

Discuss your plans with your local bank manager and the bank's international operations specialist.

Which U.S. credit cards can I use abroad?

Cards such as American Express, Diners Club, Visa, and MasterCard are recognized and accepted almost everywhere. If you have credit limits, try to have them raised to the maximum.

How do I pay my U.S. credit card bills?

Check to determine in what currency you will be billed. If you have a choice, you ought to determine whether it is more advantageous to pay in dollars or foreign currencies. Also: Be sure to notify the credit card issuers of your change of address.

How should I be prepared financially while I am traveling to my destination and while I am getting settled?

You should take credit cards, traveler's checks, and cash. Traveler's checks can be in U.S. dollars or in local currency (if available). Cash usually should be in local currency.

A sufficient number of U.S. traveler's checks in different denominations is best until you are settled. Cash them for local currency as you need them. Remember that every time you exchange money you pay a commission on the transaction.

In contrast to U.S. cash, traveler's checks generally bring a higher rate when exchanged for foreign currency.

Can I use my personal checks from home?

Sometimes, but don't rely on it. Personal checks in a foreign currency (remember, U.S. dollars are a foreign currency in another country) are not likely to be accepted. If someone knows and trusts you, that person might accept your personal check, especially if that person has a U.S. bank account into which it can be deposited.

How can I determine the proper exchange rate?

Exchange rates fluctuate with the market (unless you are in a country that has a fixed official exchange rate for U.S. dollars). These rates generally are published in newspapers. Banks that deal in foreign exchange will give you a quote at midday.

A local bank's quote could be less favorable than a

published market quote (the latter represents trades in very large amounts). However, a bank will usually give you a better rate of exchange than a hotel or business.

If you want to exchange a substantial amount of money, don't hesitate to try to negotiate a more favorable rate with the bank. If you have time, shop around. It is not wise to exchange money on the street.

If I am going to a third country, should I take dollars or local currency from the country in which I am located? Or is it better to exchange money before I go?

There is no right answer. If very large sums are involved, this can be a question of arbitrage, in which multiple exchanges are advantageous. But for the average traveler, the possibility of an arbitrage profit is remote, if only because differentials and commissions eat away at the profits.

Generally, it is more advantageous to buy a given country's currency (with dollars or another foreign currency) after you get there and to sell what you have left over after you get home. If you live abroad in country A and are visiting country B, it is best to take a small amount of cash in B's currency and the bulk of your money in dollars or country A currency, if it is easily convertible.

Every time you exchange money you pay a commission. Also, the price at which an exchange agent buys a foreign currency is always lower than the price at which that agent sells the same currency at any given moment.

A good rule: Don't transact any more exchanges than you absolutely must. If you have a small amount of a currency left from a trip or transaction, it might be less costly merely to retain it for future use. If you exchange more money than you need, you will usually lose on the reverse exchange.

Can my bank at home be helpful in establishing b[illegible] my destinations?

Even if your country of destination has a well-d[illegible] system, it might not be easy for you to establish [illegible] connections and a line of credit. Your bank at h[illegible]

Banks often provide letters of introd[illegible] would be addressed to a correspondent bank in the other country. In addition to providing a general reference, the letter can give a written guarantee for checks cashed against the home bank and provide and guarantee your signature.

Your home bank probably will set limits on the dollar value of the checks and a time limit for the guarantee (it could be as long as one year). Your bank might charge for this service in addition to requiring you to keep a balance of funds available for such transactions.

Many large U.S. banks have representatives abroad whose job is to develop business for that bank. If you are going to a place where your bank has a representative, a letter of introduction from your home bank could also be helpful.

Part of my salary is going to be paid to me in the USA. How can my home bank help me make use of this money?

Most U.S. banks now provide for direct deposit. You can arrange to have your employer and anyone else who owes you money make deposits to your account.

Your home bank can then arrange a Funds Transfer Agreement. This agreement can provide for regular transfers of funds from your account in the USA to your account abroad in a correspondent bank. In some places, the funds can be available on the same or next business day.

For irregular transfers or emergencies, the bank and you—the customer—can establish a confidential code for your use. You can then telephone or telex your request, and the code will identify you.

There are charges for these services. They are usually a ...on of a percent of the amount involved, with a minimum and a ...ximum fee. A charge also is added for the actual transmission.

Would my home bank transfer funds to me in dollars or local currency? At what rate?

This depends on the regulations in the country where you are located. If U.S. dollar accounts are permitted, your home bank can transmit dollars if you prefer. You should take into account any charges for maintaining dollar accounts and the exchange rate differentials if you plan to exchange the dollars for local currency.

If you prefer, your home bank can transmit local currency after exchanging the money in the USA. On most transactions, the rate will be the current market or spot rate. However, if your home bank deals heavily in the currency of the country where you are located, it might be possible for you to negotiate more favorable rates on substantial sums.

Personal Finances

Is there any limit on the amount of money a person can take out of the USA or bring back?

The transportation of currency or monetary instruments, regardless of the amount, is legal. However, if you take out of or bring into (or attempt to take out of or bring into) the USA more than $10,000 (U.S. or foreign equivalent or a combination of the two) in coin, currency, traveler's checks, or bearer instruments such as money orders, checks, stocks, or bonds, you are required by law to file a report on a Form 4790 with the U.S. Customs Service. If you have someone else carry the currency or instruments for you, you must also file the report.

What happens if I fail to file the required report?

Failure to file the required report or false statements on the report might lead to seizure of the currency or instruments and to civil penalties and/or criminal prosecution.

Is a U.S. citizen permitted to have a bank account abroad?

Yes, as far as the U.S. government is concerned. The host country could have restrictions or limitations, so it is a good idea to check before trying to open one.

You must file Form 90-22.1 (report of Foreign Bank and Financial Accounts) with the Treasury Department by June 30 every year to show your financial interest in a foreign bank account. Copies generally come with your tax return packages each year. There are civil and criminal penalties for failure to file.

Can a U.S. citizen have a bank account in the USA while abroad?

Yes, and it is both useful and important to have one. But choose your U.S. bank carefully.

A branch of the bank you deal with should know you well and know something about your financial affairs. It will be useful if someone there knows you well enough to take telephone instructions in a real emergency.

The bank should have a broad range of domestic and international services available at reasonable charges. Find out what these charges are in advance. The bank should have a correspondent bank in or near your location abroad.

How can I arrange to pay bills and take care of business matters at home while I am abroad?

Many banking institutions (banks, savings and loan associations, and credit unions) provide such services as your agent.

You can arrange to have funds deposited regularly in an account with instructions to pay certain items when they arise.

You can have regular creditors send your bills to your banking agent.

The banking institution might even be prepared to extend you a line of credit to pay your bills.

If so, the cost of the credit might include the charges for the service. None of the services is likely to be free, although the banking institutions have different ways of getting paid (e.g., specific charges for each service; credit charges for your line of credit; free use of your money, including a large minimum balance required between payments). Shop around, but remember that cost is only one criterion. The other is reliability.

Can't I just send checks through the mail to my creditors in the USA, making payments out of my home bank account?

Yes. However, bankers do not recommend this because of the possible delays or losses in the mail. If the mail is reliable and you can reasonably judge the time needed for mail to arrive, you should have no problems.

I own some coupon bonds, and the coupons need to be clipped and deposited periodically. Can my home bank help?

Yes. Some banks have a coupon clipping service, although it might be limited to bonds purchased through that bank. The fees for doing this usually will be nominal for securities purchased through the bank, but must be negotiated for other securities.

Will my home bank lend me money while I am abroad?

Yes, in principle. However, you will have to qualify just like any other customer of the bank. You might be able to arrange a line of credit before you go. This would be wise if you think you are going to need it.

If you want to borrow money to buy something you'll be taking with you, and the item you buy is security for the loan (e.g., an automobile), you might have a problem getting the loan because you are taking the security out of the reach of the bank. Pledging security that stays within the bank's reach could be the solution.

What about real estate loans for use abroad?

Very unlikely. However, here is where the foreign representative of your home bank could be helpful, either by arranging the loan through your home bank or by helping you find a lender abroad.

Should I involve a lawyer in the arrangement with my banking agent?

It might be useful to give a lawyer power of attorney to intervene with the banking agent in case of problems or to contact creditors who could be neglected by the banking agent. Remember, cost is a consideration, but so is reliability.

Some large employers do provide these services to employees they send abroad. These could reduce or eliminate the costs altogether. The best arrangement would be for you to choose the banking agent and lawyer yourself, and have your employer (if possible) reimburse you for the costs. That way the banking agent and lawyer are responsible directly to you for actions they take.

Housing

I own a house in the USA and when I return from abroad I expect to return to that community. What should I do about the house?

The question is whether to sell or to rent, and because everyone's situation is a little different the answer is a matter of personal judgment.

Selling is the easiest course for most people because they are relieved of managing the rental and maintenance of the property from abroad through an agent. But this is not always the wisest course.

Normally, capital gains taxes on the sale of a house are deferred if you reinvest the proceeds on a new house (whose price is at least equal to the sale price of the old house) within two years.

If a stay abroad begins before the end of the two-year

replacement period, you can have up to two more years—a total of four years—to buy a new home without paying capital gains taxes.

If you are over 55, you have the option of taking the once-in-a-lifetime $125,000 exemption on capital gains from the sale of your house if you have lived in it for three out of the past five years.

Renting has many economic advantages that could more than compensate you for its inconveniences.

New rules concerning the deductibility of losses from rental property came into effect in 1987. Before making a decision to rent your house, find out how these rules could affect you.

Many large employers who transfer their employees abroad have institutionalized arrangements for dealing with the transferred employee's house. Consult with your employer's experts before you do anything.

What should I consider before deciding whether to rent or sell my house before going abroad?

If you sell, consider:

How much is the house worth compared to what you paid?

Will you incur a loss?

Will you have capital gains that will be taxed?

How much will a comparable house cost when you return, and will you be able to afford it?

If you rent the property, consider:

Will the house be rented continuously while you are away?

Will tenant turnover be minimal?

Will rent be high enough to cover mortgage payments, taxes, insurance, maintenance costs, agent fees, and something extra for wear and some profit for you?

Will you find a reliable and reasonably priced rental agent to manage the property during your absence?

What about housing in my new location? Should I buy or rent?

In many countries outside the USA, economic and legal obstacles might eliminate any choice. You probably will be forced to rent, although buying could be an excellent decision if you have the opportunity and local law allows it.

In many foreign countries, the cost of land and housing is prohibitive to all but the wealthiest. Also, many countries put restrictions on foreigners' rights to purchase land or housing.

If you find something you like and you can afford it, it could be an excellent investment. However, before you decide to buy, check for resale restrictions.

Chapter 3

Citizenship and Nationality

Introduction

If you and all your family members were born in the USA and have lived there until now, you have no worries about citizenship and nationality.

If, during your stay abroad, neither you nor other family members change your status or voluntarily do anything that will raise questions about your citizenship, you have no worries about citizenship or nationality.

This is likely to be the situation for most people.

If you do not fit the above profile or you do not know the consequences of certain actions, you could have problems.

It is good to be informed because, even if you are only thinking about a change in family status or doing something that will integrate you more fully into your local community abroad, there are possible consequences.

Some questions do arise:

What does "USA" mean in geographic terms?

Throughout this section, it includes the states, the District of Columbia, Puerto Rico, Guam, the U.S. Virgin Islands, and outlying possessions (American Samoa and Swains Island).

Where can a person who is not a legal expert find detailed and understandable information about citizenship and nationality?

The U.S. Government Printing Office issues a bibliography that is updated periodically, entitled *Immigration, Naturalization and Citizenship*. The books it lists are also available from the Government Printing Office, but there is a charge, and only U.S. dollars are accepted.

The bibliography is available free from any GPO bookstore or from:

- Superintendent of Documents
  U.S. Government Printing Office
  Washington, DC 20402

The Bureau of Consular Affairs of the Department of State also provides information sheets on acquisition and loss of U.S. citizenship and dual nationality. The sheets are available free of charge upon written or telephone request.

What is the basic law of the USA on citizenship?

The basic statute is the Immigration and Nationality Act, which can be found in Title 8 of the United States Code (or Code Annotated).

The law includes numerous regulations based on the statute, which can be found in Title 8 of the Code of Federal Regulations, Administrative Decisions and Federal Court Decisions, including some key decisions of the U.S. Supreme Court. Moreover, the law is changing constantly as new case situations are decided and as the law is amended.

Other than being born in the USA, is there another way to become a U.S. citizen?

Yes. There are at least two other ways established by statute:

Naturalization.

By being born to U.S. citizens (with numerous qualifications and exceptions) outside the USA.

Do all countries grant citizenship by birth?

Being born in a foreign country does not always guarantee citizenship of that country. Some countries grant citizenship only to children born to citizens of that country. This is under the international law principle of *jus sanguinis* (law of inheritance by blood relationship).

If some countries grant citizenship by birth in their territory (*jus soli*) and others by blood inheritance (*jus sanguinis*), and presumably most or all countries allow citizenship by naturalization, doesn't this result in some very complicated situations? How can they be resolved?

In some cases, individuals might be without a nationality or stateless. Others might have several nationalities (dual nationals), including some they would rather not have but are unable to shed.

Are U.S. citizens permitted to be nationals of more than one country?

Yes, if it is unavoidable. But any voluntary adoption of another nationality can jeopardize the U.S. citizenship status of that person.

Does the USA require persons who become naturalized citizens to give up their other citizenships?

The USA requires naturalized citizens to renounce their foreign allegiances. However, this might not result in losing citizenship in other countries. The other country might still consider you its citizen with the obligation to fulfill your duties, such as serving in the armed forces or paying taxes.

How can the other country enforce those obligations against a U.S. citizen?

If you are a dual national (i.e., a U.S. citizen and a citizen of another country) and you go to the other country of which you are also a citizen, the other country might force you to meet your obligations as its citizen. Under international law, the U.S. government cannot protect you in such situations.

You should check before you go to see what obligations you might be called upon to meet. Also: Check to see if the USA has any special agreements (formal or informal) with the other country that deal with these situations. Check the situation for every member of your family who accompanies you because each case might be different.

A member of the family accompanying me abroad is stateless. What should I do?

Check with the Immigration and Naturalization Service (INS) to determine whether the family member can be naturalized as a U.S. citizen before departure. If your family situation permits, the stateless family member may wish to delay departure for a short period and rejoin the rest of the family abroad after naturalization.

Check with the INS to determine what needs to be done to ensure that the family member has some means of identity (if not a passport, then a *laissez-passer*) and a permit to re-enter the USA.

Check with the consulate or embassy of your country of destination to be certain of the conditions for entering and remaining there, and make sure the stateless person has the proper visa.

While you are abroad, it is advisable to make your situation known to the nearest U.S. consulate or embassy and with their assistance become known to the appropriate local authorities.

Can the U.S. Department of State be helpful in answering citizenship questions?

Yes. You might want to contact:

- Citizens Consular Services
  Room 4817
  Department of State
  Washington, DC 20520

My spouse and I are U.S. citizens. We were born in the USA and have lived there all our lives. We are expecting a child who will be born while we are abroad. What will be the citizenship of the child?

The child automatically will become a citizen of the USA. If your country of destination follows the principle of *jus soli*, the child will probably be a dual national, unless yours is an exceptional case (e.g., if you have diplomatic immunity or if a Status of Forces Agreement affecting the military applies to you). If the country of destination follows *jus sanguinis*, your child will have only one citizenship—USA.

My spouse and I are both U.S. citizens by birth, but neither of us has ever lived in the USA. What will be the U.S. citizenship status of our child born abroad?

Your child will not automatically be a U.S. citizen. Depending on the law of the country where the child is born and whether or not you or your spouse has dual citizenship, your child might be the citizen of another country or might be stateless.

In order for the child to gain automatic citizenship, one of you must have had a residence in the USA before the child was born.

I am a U.S. citizen and my spouse is an alien. Will our child born abroad be a citizen?

Yes, if you were physically present in the USA for at least 5 years, including 2 years after age 14, before the child is born.

Does any of the time I lived abroad count toward this physical presence test?

Yes. If you were abroad in the U.S. military, diplomatic, or government service or served with a public international organization recognized by the USA, or if you were the unmarried child and household member of someone else who was, then this time might count toward meeting the physical presence test.

What if my parents were in private business abroad?

That time abroad does not count.

My child, a U.S. citizen, has married an alien, and they are living abroad. If they have a child before my child is age 19, will my grandchild be a U.S. citizen?

Yes. A U.S. citizen married to an alien must be at least age 16 in order to transmit citizenship to a child born abroad.

What is the citizenship of a child who is born abroad out of wedlock, if one of the natural parents is a U.S. citizen?

Generally, the child will be considered to have acquired his or her mother's nationality at birth, under the U.S. statute, and will be a U.S. citizen if the mother is. The mother must have been previously physically present in the USA for a continuous period of at least one year before the child was born.

If the father is a U.S. citizen, and if paternity is established and the father agrees in writing to provide financial support, then the same rules apply as would apply to a child born abroad whose parents are husband and wife.

I am certain that my child born abroad is qualified to be a U.S. citizen by birth. How do I make sure that the child's right to citizenship is established?

There are three ways to establish your child's citizenship, and American Citizens Abroad recommends you pursue all of them. Two involve the Department of State. The third involves the Immigration and Naturalization Service (INS) at the Justice Department.

What citizenship documents does the Department of State issue?

First, the U.S. embassy or consulate with jurisdiction over the place of birth can issue a Consular Report of Birth Abroad and a Certification of Birth. The Consular Report of Birth is issued solely as proof of U.S. citizenship and is based on the local (foreign) birth certificate, evidence of U.S. citizenship of the parent(s), and evidence that the parent(s) complied with the applicable residence or physical presence requirements. They should be obtained in addition to and not in place of the local birth certificate. You should request these documents before the child reaches age 5, and must pay a $13 fee. If you move to another location after the child's birth, the nearest embassy or consulate can begin the Report of Birth and forward it to the embassy or consulate with jurisdiction over the place of birth for completion and issuance of the Certification of Birth.

Second, you should apply for a U.S. passport through the nearest U.S. embassy or consulate. You can do this at any age of the child, but the sooner the better.

You will need forms, photos, and supporting documents, so it is best to call ahead to find out what is needed. The child will need a passport to enter the USA without difficulty.

What citizenship document is issued by the INS?

INS issues a Certificate of Citizenship upon application on Form N-600 to the district office with jurisdiction over the applicant's place of U.S. residence. Form N-600 is intended for use in the USA but is available at some embassies and consulates or by mail from the appropriate INS district office. The applicant must provide photographs and documentary evidence of citizenship and pay a $35 fee. The applicant may have to be interviewed in person, and (unless he or she is a young child) must take an oath of allegiance to the USA. Although the person is entitled to services as a citizen upon approval of the application, the Certificate itself can only be issued while the person is in the USA. You might have to write to the INS:

- Immigration and Naturalization Service
  4420 N. Fairfax Dr.
  Arlington, VA 22203

Why do I have to deal with the INS on this matter when I already have dealt with the Department of State?

The law provides that the INS is generally responsible for determinations of citizenship within the USA and that the Department of State is responsible for determinations outside the USA. The Department of State is also solely responsible for the issuance of passports both domestically and abroad. However, since 1982, the passport and Report of Birth have been recognized by law as proof of citizenship to the same extent as documents issued by the INS. Also, the INS and the Department of State have agreed on a means to coordinate their overlapping responsibilities. It is therefore not necessary to obtain any document from one agency as proof of citizenship if you already have a document issued by the other. However, it is a good idea from a practical standpoint for a citizen born abroad to obtain a passport, Report of Birth, and Certificate of Citizenship in order to satisfy questions raised by someone who may not be aware of the applicable laws.

Where your child's long-term best interests are involved, it is best to obtain all the available documentation.

Other than citizenship by birth, how can my child qualify for citizenship?

Through naturalization. Naturalization can be accomplished either automatically through naturalization of an alien parent (if the child is a minor) or by direct petition on behalf of the child.

How does a child become automatically naturalized along with the alien spouse of a citizen?

The spouse's naturalization must occur before the child's 18th birthday. The child must also be lawfully admitted for permanent residence at the time of the spouse's naturalization and begin to reside permanently in the USA while under age 18.

How does the petition for naturalization work?

It requires a formal application, an examination of the application, and a final court hearing. The details, including requirements that must be met for children and others as well, and many special case situations, are outlined in a pamphlet, *Naturalization Requirements and General Information*, available from the Immigration and Naturalization Service.

My alien spouse served in the U.S. military. Are there any exceptions to the normal requirements for naturalization that might apply?

Yes. Some of the residence requirements may be waived. Other exceptions apply. The pamphlet mentioned in the preceding answer lists the most important ones.

Is it possible for my alien spouse to become a U.S. citizen without fulfilling the U.S. residence requirement for naturalization?

Yes, if you are a U.S. citizen and your alien spouse lives with you after applying for naturalization. Also, yes, if your work abroad is for the U.S. government, recognized U.S. research institutes, U.S. firms or subsidiaries developing foreign trade, or public international organizations. Also eligible are clergy members or missionaries affiliated with religious organizations in the USA.

Your spouse also is eligible if you will reside in the USA as soon as your foreign work ends.

The term "permanent residence" keeps cropping up. What does it mean?

Being "lawfully admitted for permanent residence" means you are given the right to enter the USA indefinitely. While you are "permanently residing" in the USA, it means you have no present intention to leave. But determining that you permanently resided there in the past is not always easy, and all the facts in each case must be examined.

My spouse and I are both U.S. citizens, and we are considering adopting an alien child while we are abroad. Can the child become a U.S. citizen?

Yes, by either of two means.

First, the child may be naturalized upon petition to a federal court by the citizen adoptive parent(s) before the child reaches age 18.

Second, the child may obtain a Certificate of Citizenship from the INS upon application by the adoptive parent(s) on the child's behalf (administrative naturalization) before the child reaches age 18.

Are there any special requirements in such cases?

Yes. The child must be adopted before age 16, be lawfully admitted for permanent residence, and have resided in the USA in the custody of the adoptive parent(s). No particular period of residence is required. Also, the child must be in the USA in order to be issued a Certificate of Citizenship under the second method.

It should be quicker and easier for most children to be issued a Certificate of Citizenship under the second method than it would be to undergo naturalization proceedings. However, some parents may prefer the formality of judicial naturalization.

What if only one adoptive parent is a citizen?

If that citizen adoptive parent is stationed abroad in the U.S. armed forces or fits one of the categories on the question of naturalizing a spouse who never lived in the USA, then the child can be naturalized without prior residence requirements. The citizen adoptive parent must declare that the child will take up residence in the USA when the employment abroad ends.

Can I lose my citizenship when I go abroad?

Yes, but it will result only from some voluntary active step you take that renounces or compromises your U.S. citizenship status. For example:

You are convicted of treason, attempting to overthrow the U.S. government, or bearing arms in a foreign army.

You renounce your U.S. citizenship before a U.S. diplomatic or consular officer following the proper formalities.

You accept or perform foreign government employment as a citizen of that country or under an oath of allegiance to it.

You enter or serve in a foreign government's armed forces as a commissioned or non-commissioned officer or during hostilities against the USA.

You swear allegiance to another country.

You voluntarily become a citizen of a foreign country.

When becoming a citizen of another country, you might unknowingly jeopardize your U.S. citizenship, even if you have no intention of renouncing that citizenship. It is best to contact the closest U.S. consulate for further information. To establish record of the fact that you intend to remain a U.S. citizen, write an official statement of intent to remain a U.S. citizen and have the document witnessed by a U.S. consular officer.

This statement may be inconsistent with an oath of allegiance to the foreign government renouncing U.S. citizenship or allegiance to the USA, or with other statements made to the foreign authorities. You should try to be exempted from making such statements and provide documentary evidence of your efforts to the consular officer. You should also maintain and document official ties to the USA by maintaining a current U.S. passport, U.S. voter registration, and filing of U.S. tax returns.

Be informed of all the complications before taking any steps that might jeopardize your citizenship.

What if I became a naturalized foreign citizen involuntarily, such as through my parents when I was a minor? Will I lose my U.S. citizenship?
Foreign naturalization through parents is no longer ground for possible loss of U.S. citizenship.

If I vote in a foreign election, will I lose my citizenship?
Not according to present law and if it is legal for you to do so under the foreign country's laws.

Do children born abroad with citizenship have to return to the USA to preserve it?
Not according to present law.

Will required military service in a foreign country cause loss of U.S. citizenship, as in the case of a dual national?
Not necessarily. To be certain, the individual can request permission from both the secretary of state and the secretary of defense, but this is rarely done.

Another approach that seems to help is for the individual to protest induction in writing to the authorities. If the protest is rejected, the written protest is clear evidence that the inductee did not serve voluntarily.

As previously stated, the person's statements or conduct must establish intention to relinquish U.S. citizenship.

Chapter 4

Taxation at Home and Abroad

Introduction

Citizens of the USA living abroad continue to have U.S. tax obligations.

However, it is difficult to determine what is owed. If you prepare your own tax returns in the USA, you might be able to figure out your tax obligation abroad, but do not count on it.

If you have paid someone else to prepare your taxes for you, be prepared to continue to do so when you go abroad, but be prepared for a higher fee. These fees can run into four digits if your finances are just slightly complicated.

These rules will let you know about where you stand on U.S. taxes:

- If you are a U.S. citizen or a resident alien and meet the minimum income requirements, you must file a U.S. income tax return, even if you are liable for income tax in the foreign country in which you work.

- If you are paid by a U.S. employer, you are subject to U.S. withholding tax. If you are not subject to withholding, you must pay quarterly estimated taxes.
- Your taxes must be paid in full by April 15 following the close of the taxable year if you, like most taxpayers, are on a calendar-year basis. This is applicable even if you are entitled to a delay in filing your tax return or are granted filing extensions.
- Most importantly, some of the income you earn from working abroad (even if it is paid to you in the USA) is tax free, but there is a dollar limit. You must meet certain strict conditions about the period you live or work abroad. The rest of your income is taxable.
- Your U.S. tax liability could change even after the return is filed and the tax is paid. Often the change is in your favor, such as if you have carryback foreign tax credits (see page 42). So you must be aware of the need to file amended returns and of the deadlines.

As a U.S. citizen, I am "subject to" U.S. income taxes while I am living abroad. Can you explain?

In principle, you are subject to federal income taxes on all your income from whatever source (worldwide). Under some circumstances, you might be subject to state income taxes if you are a resident of a particular state. This does not mean you will owe taxes. Why? Because there are some important exemptions and deductions that apply to citizens and resident aliens living abroad. But if you have any appreciable amount of income, you must file income tax returns. Ordinarily, being "subject to" taxes means you must file a tax return whether you owe taxes or not. It is safest to assume you must file a return unless you are certain you are not required to do so.

…get the details about my federal tax obligations while

…n No. 54, *Tax Guide for U.S. Citizens Abroad*, is an official and authoritative source for the average citizen. However, there are many nuances it does not contain. It is revised annually, so be sure you have the latest version. Write to:

- Assistant Commissioner (International)
  Internal Revenue Service
  950 L'Enfant Plaza
  Washington, DC 20024

Where can I get firsthand information about U.S. taxes while I'm abroad?
The Internal Revenue Service maintains some offices abroad. As listed in IRS Publication 54, they are in: Bonn, West Germany; Caracas, Venezuela; Riyadh, Saudi Arabia; London, England; Manila, Philippines; Mexico City, Mexico; Nassau, Bahamas; Ottawa, Canada; Paris, France; Rome, Italy; Sao Paulo, Brazil; Singapore; Sydney, Australia; and Tokyo, Japan.

If you cannot reach any of these, you should seek out the nearest office of a U.S. law firm specializing in taxes or a U.S. accounting firm. This is costly, but it might save you more in the long run. If the IRS gives you incorrect advice or information, the federal government cannot be held accountable.

Which federal tax benefits should persons living abroad be aware of?
The principal ones are:

- The Foreign Earned Income Exclusion.
- The Housing Exclusion or Deduction.
- The Foreign Tax Credit.

What is the Foreign Earned Income Exclusion?
This permits a qualified person to exclude from taxable income a specified amount of income earned during residence or presence

abroad. The amount has varied in recent years. The current maximum per-year exclusion is fixed at $70,000.

Does this apply to investment income?

The Foreign Earned Income Exclusion does not apply to investment income.

Who is qualified for the Foreign Earned Income Exclusion?

Any U.S. citizen or permanent U.S. resident alien who:

- Has foreign-earned income.
- Has a tax home in a foreign country.
- Is either a bona fide resident of a foreign country for an uninterrupted period that includes at least an entire tax year, or is physically present in a foreign country or countries for at least 330 full days during any period of 12 consecutive months.

How do I determine if I am a qualified U.S. resident alien while I work abroad?

See IRS Publication 519, *U.S. Tax Guide for Aliens.*

My spouse is not a U.S. citizen and has never lived in the USA. How does this affect my federal tax status?

You might choose to have your spouse treated as a resident alien for tax purposes. In that case, you might file a joint tax return. Once you make the choice you will be limited by law from changing the status of your spouse for tax purposes. So the choice must be made carefully and with some foresight.

What is a tax home?

Generally, your tax home is your main place of business or post of duty, regardless of where you maintain your family home. If you do not have a regular place of business, your tax home is where you regularly live.

What makes me a bona fide resident of a foreign country?

Each case is determined separately and is a question of fact. But generally, if you go to a foreign country for an indefinite or extended period and you set up permanent quarters there for yourself and your family, you probably meet the test even though you intend eventually to return to the USA. You will not qualify, however, if you deny to local authorities that you are a resident there, and they accept your denial.

The IRS will make a determination in your case on the basis of the information on the Form 2555 that you file along with your income tax return to get a foreign income exclusion.

Will voting by absentee ballot in the USA prevent me from being a bona fide resident in a foreign country?

No. However, voting in state elections in the USA can affect your liability to state taxes in some states.

When I go abroad, and my family eventually joins me, we will live in a small community provided by my employer. My employer requires this so that we can be close to my work. Does this affect my income tax liability?

Yes, it might. There are special rules for excluding the value of housing in this type of situation. This area is called a "camp" if the housing:

- Is provided for your employer's convenience because you work in a remote area where satisfactory housing is not otherwise available.
- Is located as close as is practical to the work site.
- Is not available to the general public and houses at least 10 employees.

You should investigate carefully if your situation resembles this.

I am a U.S. government employee. Am I affected by these exemptions and deductions when I work abroad?

Generally, no. You are treated like U.S. citizens at home with some exceptions. Some of your cost-of-living and foreign area allowances are excludable from gross income, but wage differentials are not. You should see IRS Publication 516, *Tax Information for U.S. Government Civilian Employees Stationed Abroad.*

I am paid by the U.S. government, but I am not a government employee. Do I qualify for the exclusions and deductions?

Yes.

Are all U.S. taxpayers abroad subject to the same tax rules?

No. There are numerous categories. Most of our discussion pertains to self-employed or privately employed individuals. Employees of the U.S. government are taxed differently, as noted previously. Members of the armed forces and some civilian employees of the armed forces are treated slightly differently from other U.S. government employees.

Still other rules apply to taxpayers in U.S. possessions, such as Guam, or who work for certain international organizations.

Even in the private sector, differences occur from country to country because of distinctions in U.S. tax laws or because of modifications in the general U.S. tax law caused by double-tax treaties.

How does the Foreign Housing Exclusion or Deduction affect my taxes?

You might claim an exclusion or a deduction for the cost of your housing beyond a "base amount" if you have a tax home in a foreign country and you qualify under either the bona fide residence test or the physical presence test. There are some strict limits, and the computation is very complex. The base amount for 1988 was $7,322, so only housing expenses above that figure could give rise to an exclusion or deduction. You will probably need some experienced help to determine this.

What housing expenses are considered?

Rent (or fair market value of housing provided by your employer), repairs, utilities, insurance, furniture rental, and parking costs are examples. Lavish expenses are not included. Neither are deductible property taxes and interest, the cost of buying property, or the cost of servants.

Can I claim the housing deduction or exclusion for two foreign households if I cannot take my family to my new post because of adverse conditions, and I install them near enough so I can visit them fairly regularly?

Yes. Under these circumstances, expenses for the second household may be included in your reasonable foreign housing expenses.

What is the difference between the housing exclusion and the housing deduction?

The housing exclusion is generally available to employed individuals. This exclusion can come only from "employer-provided amounts." Employees can claim this exclusion whether or not their employer provides them with a housing allowance or supplement.

The housing deduction is generally available only to self-employed individuals. In this case, you might deduct qualified housing expenses in excess of the base amount in figuring your adjusted gross income. It is possible in complex cases that you will be required to allocate a portion of your housing amount to the exclusion and a portion to the deduction, so familiarize yourself with the details of each.

What is the Foreign Tax Credit, and how can it affect me?

As a resident of a foreign country, you might be obligated to pay income taxes there. The extent of your obligation will be determined by local law and by any tax treaties or agreements between the USA and that country. But if you must pay something, you might take a credit against the taxes you owe to the USA.

Does that mean I can take a credit for all my foreign taxes?

Not necessarily. The taxes must qualify as income taxes and must be legitimately owed and paid. Foreign social security contributions are creditable in some cases.

Can I take advantage of the Foreign Earned Income Exclusion and the Foreign Tax Credit?

Yes, but not on the same income. If the income qualifies for the exclusion and you use it, you cannot take a credit for the foreign taxes paid on that income. But if you pay foreign tax on income that does not qualify for the exclusion, then you might take the credit against any U.S. taxes due on that income.

Is it possible to use the foreign income tax as a deduction instead of a credit if it would be more advantageous?

Yes. You have a choice, but you must use it entirely as a deduction or entirely as a credit. You can claim a deduction only for foreign income taxes paid on income that is subject to U.S. tax. You cannot claim a deduction for foreign taxes paid on income excluded under the Foreign Earned Income Exclusion or under the housing exclusion.

Can I deduct other kinds of foreign taxes in figuring my U.S. tax?

Yes, real property taxes. However, personal property and sales taxes are deductible only as business or income-producing expenses. These are in addition to the foreign tax credit for foreign income taxes.

Because of the differences between the taxable year in the USA and in the country where I live, I cannot be certain now that the choices I make regarding tax credits or tax deductions are the best ones for me. Can I change my mind?

Yes. You can file an amended return within three years of the due date of the return in question or within two years of the date you paid the U.S. tax.

Apart from the special exclusions for foreign earned income, will I apply the rest of the U.S. tax rules the same way I did in the USA?

No. Unfortunately, large numbers of U.S. tax provisions draw a distinction between taxpayers inside and outside the USA. In many cases, this is an economic disincentive to living and working abroad.

For example, contributions to foreign charities generally cannot be deducted; and foreign property depreciates more slowly than U.S. property.

When is my federal income tax return due if I live abroad?

If you live outside the USA, or travel outside the USA for 14 continuous days, including April 15 (the normal due date), you get an automatic extension to June 15. Additional delays are possible but must be requested. (See the tax calendar at the end of this chapter.)

Can I also delay payment of the tax?

Any taxes due but not paid by April 15 will incur interest charges.

Where do I file my return from abroad?

- IRS Service Center
  Philadelphia, PA 19255

What are the principal forms that I must file?

Everyone files Form 1040. To qualify for the Foreign Earned Income Exclusion, you must also file Form 2555 every year. If you need more time to file your returns, Form 2350 is a special form to request an extension of time for U.S. citizens or residents abroad who would like to delay filing until after they meet the bona fide residence or physical presence test.

What if I want to appeal an adverse ruling on my taxes?

Abroad, you have the same rights as if you were in the USA. You might be able to arrange an appeals conference abroad, but any further appeal must be made to the U.S. courts in the USA.

Where can the IRS take action against me?

Only in the USA, including the District of Columbia and U.S. territories.

Can I pay my taxes in foreign currency?

Generally, no. Only U.S. currency is acceptable.

My foreign income is paid to me in local currency. How do I report it?

You must report in U.S. dollars converted at a realistic rate of exchange (official rate or open market rate or some other rate). But you must be able to justify the rate you use.

Can I contribute to an Individual Retirement Account (IRA) while I am working abroad?

Yes, but only on income that is includable in your gross income. Thus, income that is excluded under the Foreign Earned Income Exclusion cannot qualify for an IRA deduction. However, even if you work abroad, income from a business in the USA or even earnings abroad that exceed the exclusion might be used for an IRA.

I understand that Congress has amended the gift and estate tax law to increase the tax burden when the estate of a U.S. citizen passes to a spouse who is an alien. Is this correct? Please explain.

Congress has created a distinction in U.S. gift and estate tax rules so that a U.S. citizen who makes gifts to an alien spouse, or whose estate passes at death to an alien spouse, is treated less favorably than if the spouse is a U.S. citizen. For this purpose, the new rules, which took effect Jan. 1, 1989, treat resident and non-resident aliens alike. The marital deduction is available only if the spouse is a U.S. citizen. Thus, U.S. citizens can make unlimited lifetime gifts and unlimited transfers-at-death to a U.S. citizen spouse without incurring gift or estate taxes.

Moreover, they can make up to $600,000 of non-spousal gifts/transfers without incurring gift or estate taxes.

But when the spouse is an alien, all lifetime gifts to that spouse (in excess of the annual exclusion) and all transfers-at-death are taxable unless they are treated as part of the $600,000 that U.S. citizens can give away or transfer at death without tax.

The new law contains a planning feature of potential importance for U.S. citizens who die with wealth in excess of the $600,000 of property that passes on without tax. The marital deduction can be preserved for the benefit of the alien spouse so long as the property that passes to the alien spouse is placed in a "qualified domestic trust." Such a trust must have U.S. trustees, all the income must be payable to the surviving spouse, the trust must meet certain rules to ensure that estate tax will ultimately be collected from the trust, and a choice must be made on the estate tax return.

Tax Calendar

January 1

- Tax year begins for individuals who are on a calendar year.
- "Entire taxable year" begins, which must be included in the uninterrupted period of bona fide residence in foreign country(ies) to qualify for the Internal Revenue Code (IRC) Section 911 Foreign Earned Income Exclusion (FEIE).

January 15

- Deadline for final payment of estimated federal income tax and for filing last voucher of Form 1040 ES, *Estimated Tax for Individuals.*

January 31

- You can avoid the January 15 deadline for payment of estimated taxes if you file your final return and pay the final taxes by Jan. 31. U.S. citizens abroad who qualify for

FEIE probably will not be able to meet this deadline. Others might.

April 15

Payment Deadlines:

- Any unpaid income tax due, regardless of when your Form 1040 is filed.
- One-fourth of current year estimated tax is due.
- Deadline for opening an Individual Retirement Account (IRA) and making deposits for the previous tax year.

Filing Deadlines:

- Date for filing Form 1040 unless there has been an extension. A gift tax return is filed with Form 1040, including extensions.
- Deadline to file for extension of time to file Form 1040 if automatic extension to June 15 is not applicable.
- Deadline for amending tax return for the third previous tax year.
- Deadline for amending foreign tax credits for the 10th previous tax year.

June 15

- Second payment on current year's estimated tax is due.
- Deadline for filing the previous year's income tax return for persons who qualified for the automatic two-month extension because they were living or traveling abroad on April 15.
- Deadline for requesting a further extension of time to file the previous year's tax return (using Form 4868) until August 15.

June 30

- Deadline for filing report on foreign financial or bank accounts with Treasury Department on Form 90-22.1.

August 15

- Deadline for filing the previous year's tax return for persons who filed Form 4868 by June 15 and were already eligible for the automatic extension to June 15.

September 15

- Third payment on current year's estimated tax is due.

December 31

- End of taxable year for calendar-year taxpayers. Last day of "entire taxable year" for FEIE purposes.

Chapter 5

Social Security

Introduction

Social Security, in one form or another, exists in most countries. However, most other countries' programs differ from U.S. programs in the type of protection provided, how it is provided, and in the degree of protection.

When most U.S. citizens think of Social Security, they think first about the amounts withheld from their wages and salaries under the label FICA. This stands for Federal Insurance Contributions Act, another name for Chapter 21 of the Internal Revenue Code. It is the basis for the U.S. tax to support the Social Security pension system.

There are many other forms of protection that fall under the heading of Social Security. Some of these exist in the USA. Even more exist in other industrialized countries.

Almost every country in the world has the equivalent of

what U.S. citizens know as workers' compensation, though they might call it employment injury and occupational disease insurance.

Second most popular is the pension sector, known as old age survivors' and disability (most countries call it invalidity) benefits.

Third in popularity is the sickness and health insurance sector where programs are designated as cash sickness benefits, medical care insurance, and maternity benefits. These exist in the USA, but—except for Medicare—are not thought of as Social Security because they are provided for mostly through private insurance, not government programs.

Family allowances (sometimes called children's allowances) and unemployment insurance programs exist mainly in industrialized countries. Family allowances, which have no real equivalent in the USA, are also found in some developing countries, particularly those that have been influenced heavily by France. These last two programs present some special problems for aliens and temporary workers in the countries where they are provided.

When I go abroad to work, what happens to my U.S. Social Security? Do I continue paying? Will my protection continue?

No single answer to any of these questions fits every case. A lot will depend on your present individual circumstances and your past work history. It will also depend on who your employer is while you are abroad or whether you are self-employed.

I am a U.S. citizen, and my employer is a company based in the USA. How does this affect my situation?

If you are a U.S. citizen or even a permanent resident of the USA and your employer is a U.S. employer as defined by law (most U.S. companies meet this legal criterion), your work abroad will be subject to FICA. You will get protection just as though you had never left the USA.

Your employer will withhold your contributions from your salary and pay an equal amount.

What if my U.S. employer sends me to work for a foreign subsidiary abroad?

You will be in the same position as someone who works directly for your U.S. employer, if the employer has an agreement with the Internal Revenue Service to cover U.S. citizens working for that subsidiary. This is often called a 3121(1) agreement because it is authorized under Section 3121(1) of the Internal Revenue Code.

What if there is no 3121(1) agreement for that subsidiary?

You might still be covered if it can be clearly established that your employer is really the U.S. employer, not the subsidiary.

Here, common-law rules of employer-employee relationships must be applied carefully. The essential question that must be answered is, "Who has the ultimate right to control your work?" Many facts can bear on the answer to this question, but it is the right to control, not the actual exercise of control, that is essential in determining who is your employer.

The country where I am going to work also has a social security program and a tax to support it. Am I required to pay that also?

Ordinarily, yes. But there might be some exceptions.

The law of the country might exclude foreigners who work there for a short time or for an initial period of, say, one year. Or there might be grounds for exclusion under a treaty or international social security agreement. This is something your employer—or you, if self-employed—should investigate.

If my foreign employer abroad has no connection with the USA, can I make voluntary contributions to U.S. Social Security (i.e., FICA)?

No. Voluntary contributions to U.S. Social Security are not permitted under any circumstances.

I'm self-employed abroad. Must I report my income for Social Security purposes in the USA?

Yes. If you are a U.S. citizen or permanent resident of the USA and have self-employment income from activities abroad, you must report and pay the SECA tax (SECA stands for Self-Employment Contributions Act or Chapter 2 of the Internal Revenue Code). This is true even if your income for income tax purposes qualifies for the Foreign Earned Income Exclusion, which is not applicable for Social Security tax purposes.

Ministers of religion should take particular note of this. They are considered self-employed for U.S. Social Security purposes and must report as such even though they may actually be employees.

Do so-called "totalization agreements" have an effect on where I owe Social Security taxes and where I get protection?

Yes. But the number of these agreements is limited at the present time, and they also affect benefit rights. They will be discussed more fully in answers to some later questions.

If I stop paying U.S. Social Security taxes when I go abroad, or if my employer stops deducting FICA from my salary and doesn't pay the tax, what happens to my protection?

If there is an obligation to pay but no payment is made, the matter is treated by the IRS like any other tax delinquency. Interest and penalties accrue. Criminal charges might be added.

Nevertheless, if the work is legitimately covered by U.S. Social Security, even though no tax has been paid, quarters of coverage will accrue and protection will be maintained. Normally, the obligation to pay both the employer's and employee's share of FICA is that of the employer. The employer merely collects the employee's share. The employee is not penalized if the employer fails to live up to the legal obligation.

It's a good idea for every employed or self-employed person who is covered by Social Security to check the records periodically, at least every third taxable year. This provides an opportunity to correct errors and avoid the statute of limitation, which under some circumstances could prevent correction of records.

In order to obtain an update of your record of payment of Social Security taxes while abroad, contact the U.S. consulate in your country of residence. The consulate can provide a form, which you should fill out and send to the address on the back of the form.

Social Security will then process the information and return the form to you.

What if the tax payments stop because there is no further coverage or obligation to pay? Does this mean I no longer have any protection?
Not necessarily. But it does mean that your protection under the U.S. program will not increase and might decrease and eventually vanish if you remain outside covered employment long enough.

Am I eligible to receive benefits while living outside the USA?
Yes. If you are a U.S. citizen and are qualified to receive a benefit while you are living abroad, you will receive your benefits. There are a few countries to which benefits cannot be sent. They are: Albania, Kampuchea (formerly Cambodia), Cuba, East Germany, North Korea, and Vietnam. But benefits accrue to U.S. citizens who are in those countries, and these benefits are paid to them when they leave.

Might I receive a railroad retirement benefit, a Civil Service retirement annuity, a Foreign Service retirement annuity, or a military service pension abroad?
Yes.

Medicare

If I retire abroad, what happens to my Medicare protection?
Your protection remains valid but only for treatment in the USA.

Is there any way I can get Medicare benefits outside the USA?

Ordinarily, no. There are a few exceptions for people who get sick in the USA if the closest available adequate care is outside the country, as in Canada or Mexico.

Because I am retiring abroad, does it make any sense for me to participate in Part B of Medicare (Supplementary Medical Insurance), which requires a monthly premium?

The answer depends on your plans and circumstances. If there is a chance you will return to the USA eventually, even if it is only to obtain medical treatment, it would be worth considering.

If you fail to subscribe to Part B when you are first entitled to do so, you must wait until the next open season (January–March each year). The cost gets higher each time you pass an open season without subscribing. Your protection begins on the July 1 following the open season. Therefore, it could take anywhere from 3 months to 15 months between your decision to subscribe and the effective date of the protection. If you return to the USA during that period, you will have a problem.

Jobless Benefits

Am I protected by unemployment insurance in the USA while I am working abroad?

If you are working directly for a U.S. employer based in the USA, the answer most likely is yes. But you must return to the USA to apply, and you must again be available for work in the USA. Canada is an exception to this rule. You can apply and receive benefits there under an agreement between the two countries.

What if my employer is a foreign company?

Theoretically, you probably will have some rights in the local unemployment insurance system if there is one. However, as a practical matter, if you become unemployed, you might not be permitted to remain in the country if you are there only as a temporary resident.

Once you leave the country, it is unlikely you will be able to export any unemployment benefits. There might be a few exceptions to this from time to time when a country wants to encourage its temporary alien workers to relocate elsewhere.

Workers' Compensation

Where will my workers' compensation protection come from if I'm working abroad and I'm injured at work?

If you are working in another country at your employer's place of business, you will most likely be protected under the local system. The benefits usually will include medical treatment, as well as temporary replacement of at least a portion of your lost salary. Permanent injury compensation claims, like those in the USA, are also possible in some countries.

If you are working for a U.S. company, you might be able to fall back on the employer's insurance in the USA. Some states require this, so it depends on where your employer's place of business is located in the USA.

You are not likely to be able to collect from several sources because, while many foreign systems are quite liberal in providing immediate care and compensation, they are also quite strict about not duplicating benefits.

What is the effect of Social Security totalization agreements, which coordinate benefits and employee payments between the USA and other countries?

If there is such an agreement between the USA and the country where you are working, it generally will have an effect on your coverage and on any future benefits.

If you would be covered in both countries without an agreement, the agreement will provide for eliminating one of the coverages (and accompanying contributions or taxes). If you have credits in both countries, the credits from one can be used if necessary by the other, under the agreement, to establish your entitlement. Once you become entitled in this manner, you generally will receive a benefit —that would not otherwise have been possible—based on the credits earned in the paying country.

You might get several benefits (partial ones to be sure): one from each country where you have some credits, but not enough to be entitled without combining credits from the other country or countries. Of course, if you have enough credits without combining, you will get a benefit as you would otherwise. Agreements also have the effect of eliminating various obstacles to the export of benefits from one country to another.

What kind of benefits are affected by agreements between the USA and other countries?

They include Social Security taxes and retirement, disability benefits, and survivors insurance benefits.

With which countries does the USA have agreements?

Belgium, Canada, France, Italy, Norway, Spain, Sweden, Switzerland, the United Kingdom, and West Germany.

What happens to my U.S. Social Security if I go abroad to work for an international organization?

You are not covered by U.S. Social Security while you are outside the USA. If you are sent back to the USA to work, even for a short time, that work and the earnings attributable to it are covered and subject to taxation as self-employment income. The international organization must be one that is recognized by the United States under the International Organization Immunities Act.

I am a beneficiary of U.S. Social Security, and I'm moving abroad. What do I need to know in order to make sure my checks continue to be sent to me?

You should notify your local Social Security Administration office of your new address, and when you arrive you should also notify the nearest U.S. embassy or consulate because in many countries they will be responsible for forwarding your checks to you. Of course, you can have your checks deposited directly in a U.S. bank account, but remember it is somewhat costly to have funds transferred abroad. Your benefits are always paid in dollars, and you will have to take care of the conversion to the currency of the country where you are living. You also should become familiar with any local currency regulations that might affect transfers of funds.

Are there any other special rules that will apply to me while living abroad?

Yes, two in particular:

First, you have to make regular reports on your status on a special form that is mailed to you either each year or every other year. If the form is not completed and returned, your benefits will be suspended. If you move, notify your nearest U.S. embassy or consulate so that your check mailing address will be changed.

Second, if you are under age 70, there are special rules about how work abroad affects your continuing right to receive benefits. You can receive all benefits due you, if your earnings do not exceed the annual exempt amount. This limit changes each year. For 1989, beneficiaries aged between 62 and 65 could earn $6,480. Recipients between 65 and 69 could earn $8,880 without sacrificing benefits.

However, if the work you are doing requires that you pay U.S. Social Security taxes, then the effect of the work on your benefit is the same as it would be if you were in the USA.

Uniformed Services

Several programs provide benefits abroad to members of the uniformed services, persons who are retired from them, veterans, and their families. There are strict limitations, so not everyone in these categories is entitled to benefits in every case. Here are the most important and most common case situations for U.S. citizens living abroad, and the most important limitations.

What constitutes the "uniformed services"?

"Uniformed services" include the Army, Navy, Marine Corps, Air Force, Coast Guard, and the Commissioned Corps of the U.S. Public Health Service (USPHS) and the National Oceanic and Atmospheric Administration (NOAA).

What kinds of programs are available?

The most important are health delivery programs. There are also several cash benefit and GI educational benefit programs. They are:

Uniformed Services Health Benefits Program (USHBP), which consists of uniformed services medical facilities, and CHAMPUS (Civilian Health and Medical Program of the Uniformed Services).

Veterans Administration (VA) programs, which include CHAMPVA (Civilian Health and Medical Program of the Veterans Administration), VA GI Educational Benefits, and VA Compensation and Pension Benefits.

Are GI home loans available for homes abroad?

No.

What does USHBP provide?

USHBP provides available care in a uniformed service medical facility for eligible civilians.

What does CHAMPUS provide?

CHAMPUS provides a share of the cost of civilian medical care when care is not available in a uniformed service facility.

Does Medicare eligibility disqualify a person for CHAMPUS?

Yes, either at age 65 or, earlier, because of a total disability or chronic kidney condition.

It is enough that a person is eligible for Medicare (Part A). It is immaterial that the person has not applied or is living abroad where Medicare benefits are not available.

What if I am over age 65 and not eligible for Medicare?

You can continue CHAMPUS eligibility if you can produce a "Notice of Disallowance" from the Social Security Administration. This means you must apply and be turned down.

Where do I apply for Medicare when I am abroad?

At any U.S. consulate. Ask for the person responsible for federal benefits. The same person is usually responsible for VA benefits as well.

What does CHAMPVA provide for eligible U.S. citizens abroad?

The same benefits as those received in the USA. Overseas CHAMPVA is administered by CHAMPUS. Application should be made to the closest U.S. military facility or the nearest U.S. embassy or consulate.

Will the VA pay for care to veterans with non-service-connected disabilities abroad?

No. However, such care is offered at the Veterans Memorial Medical Center in Manila on a space-available basis if the veteran cannot afford other hospitalization.

Are VA compensations and pension checks sent abroad?

Yes, to most locations.

Are VA (GI Bill) educational benefits available abroad?

Yes, but generally a program outside the USA may be pursued only at a VA-approved institution of higher learning.

Chapter 6

Education Abroad

Introduction

No single issue is likely to have more impact on you and your family than the education of your school-age children if you are going to live and work abroad.

Choices abound, but the variety of circumstances, personalities, needs, interests, and intellects makes the decision process bewildering. Each family must make a decision based on its own concerns and the best interests of its own children.

Educational opportunities are different from those in the USA, not necessarily in quality, but in philosophy or curriculum. For many children this can be an exhilarating experience.

What choices are there for educating children when a family goes to live or work abroad?

There are two main choices:

Take the children along and educate them abroad.

Leave them at home either in the school they are already attending or in a different school, such as a boarding school.

What contributes to those choices?

Location will determine what is available. In some locations there might be only local schools, or international schools that do not include U.S.-style curricula. Among those that do not, there might be some in which English is not even used as a working language.

Another choice is to send the child to a suitable boarding school in another part of the same country or in a nearby country.

What are some important considerations for choosing whether my child should enter a local or U.S./international school abroad?

Here are some suggested considerations:

Local schools abroad are as varied as the countries you might go to. If you like the idea of sending your child to a neighborhood school, you will simply have to look at the school before you decide whether it is suitable. Consider whether the curriculum meets your expectations or, if not, whether the opportunity to learn a foreign working language offsets other shortcomings.

The move to new surroundings affects some children more than others. Think of your child's ability and willingness to adapt to a different school system.

The child's age is an important factor on the secondary school level. The closer he or she is to preparing for college the more difficult it is to shift to a different curriculum and still meet U.S. admissions requirements.

Check whether local upper schools offer special classes for foreign students that help them with language skills before integrating them into regular classes. Completion of secondary school abroad, through the 13th school year and leading to the International Baccalaureate (a two-year, pre-university diploma program), might earn your child admission to a U.S. college at sophomore level.

Does the child have special learning needs or difficulties? Instruction in a foreign language adds an extra burden for students with reading disabilities, perceptual problems, or hearing handicaps. U.S.-style schools abroad might be able to provide more help for children with learning disabilities, but even these schools often cannot meet such children's needs.

Resources generally are not sufficient for children with severe problems, in which case a boarding school at home or in England might offer more satisfactory educational opportunities. It is advisable to check ahead to determine whether your child's needs can be met at your location abroad and to consider alternative programs such as CHAMPUS (see Chapter 5, "Social Security"), if accessible.

What is an "international school"?

These are schools that cater to a generally English-speaking international student population. They usually offer a diversified curriculum, incorporating aspects of both the British and U.S. systems.

They may vary in size from very small with few grades to all grades, kindergarten through 12. Some may offer preparation for the International Baccalaureate or the European Baccalaureate.

In the upper grades the teachers tend to be mainly U.S. citizens preparing students for higher education in the USA.

The following services might be helpful:

The Department of State's Office of Overseas Schools, which publishes a directory of *Overseas American-Sponsored Elementary and Secondary Schools Assisted by the U.S. Department of State* and a fact sheet on each of the listed schools. Write:

- Office of Overseas Schools
  A/OS, Room 234, SA-6
  U.S. Department of State
  Washington, DC 20520
  (202) 875-6220

The European Council of International Schools also publishes a directory that includes a number of U.S. colleges and universities associated with the council, as well as affiliated schools. Write:

- European Council of International Schools
  18 Lavant Street
  Petersfield, Hampshire GU32 3EW
  England

Are there any schools in foreign countries that adhere to a U.S. curriculum?

The Department of Defense runs more than 300 schools around the world. They offer a traditional U.S. curriculum, grades K–12. In rare instances they offer the International Baccalaureate.

Department of Defense Dependents Schools are tuition-free for military dependents. Children of other government employees also are admitted but must pay tuition.

Children of other U.S. citizens and of foreign nationals pay tuition and can be accepted only if space is available and if their attendance does not contravene local law.

To find out whether there is a school in your area, to request a fact sheet, and to check whether space is available, contact:

- Director
  Department of Defense
  Office of Dependents Schools
  2461 Eisenhower Ave.
  Alexandria, VA 22331-1100
  (202) 325-0188 or 325-0867

Do other countries operate schools abroad?

The British and French communities or embassies sponsor a number of schools in foreign countries. Many of the British schools see their students through primary grades only, expecting them to go to boarding school at age 11. French schools, on the other hand, might offer up to 10 or even all 13 grades, ending with the Baccalaureate.

While attendance at a French school requires learning how to speak French, this might be more useful than learning the language spoken in your new home and in the local schools.

I would like my children to share the experience of living abroad, but there are no schools where I am going. Are there any other options?

There are at least two more options:

Boarding schools, if not in the country to which you are going, then perhaps in a neighboring country, and in any case in England.

Home study correspondence programs are offered by the Calvert School (elementary) and the University of Nebraska (grades 9–12).

While we are abroad, my children will be preparing to enter a U.S. college and will want to take the Scholastic Aptitude Tests and Achievement Tests. Is that possible? Where do we obtain information?

Yes, it is possible. The *International Edition, Student Bulletin for the SAT and Achievement Tests*, published by the College Board, contains a list of testing centers abroad.

The College Board also issues a special leaflet, *Special Information for Students Who Plan to Take the SAT or Achievement Tests in Overseas Test Centers*. There is a processing fee of $13 if the test is taken in foreign countries other than Canada or Mexico.

Write:

- College Board ATP
  Box 6200
  Princeton, NJ 08541

Can my child receive a U.S. college education while living abroad?
Yes. A number of U.S. colleges abroad are listed in the European Council of International Schools directory.

How is my child's education paid for abroad?
Generally, you pay for it. This is true in some countries even when the child goes to the local schools. In many countries, free public education is not available, or at least not above certain levels.

Major employers, recognizing that education is often an added expense for their employees abroad, provide education allowances or pay for education.

Is the cost of educating my children abroad tax deductible?
No, but some educational allowances are not taxable.

What consideration can we expect on tuition from the state university in the state where we used to live?
Each state policy varies. Generally, however, universities are becoming very strict about who is qualified for lower state residents' tuition.

Normally, they require that the student has established a bona fide in-state residence over a substantial period (often a year or more) before entering the university, and not solely for the purpose of going to the university.

However, if you have regularly lived in a state, still own a residence there, or pay state income taxes, your children have a better chance of qualifying for in-state tuition.

It is not a good idea to try to obtain resident status by

doubtful means. States are not above prosecuting such cases, which could have unfortunate consequences for both parents and students.

Who recruits for teaching positions abroad?

Try the following:

- International Schools Services
  15 Rozel Road
  P.O. Box 5910
  Princeton, NJ 08543
  (609) 452-0990

- Department of Defense
  Office of Dependents Schools
  Teacher Recruitment Branch
  Room 112 Hoffman Bldg. No. 1
  2461 Eisenhower Ave.
  Alexandria, VA 22331-1100
  (202) 325-0885

Chapter 7

Consular Services Abroad

Introduction

It is hard to imagine any more unpleasant situation than being in a strange place when personal adversity strikes and not knowing how to cope or from whom to seek advice and assistance.

Don't expect the U.S. government to provide aid and assistance in every situation. On the other hand, getting acquainted and building a friendly relationship with U.S. government representatives in your vicinity is worthwhile.

Americans in trouble should head for the consular services branch of the nearest U.S. embassy or consulate. If the consulate officers there can help you, they will. If they cannot, they will try to refer you to someone who can.

U.S. citizens abroad should know that, while there is usually a consular section at a U.S. embassy, consular offices are also located elsewhere in cities where there are large concentrations of U.S. citizens or important U.S. business or commercial interests.

The differences between an embassy and a consulate office are worth remembering.

An embassy represents one government to another. The U.S. ambassador is the president's official representative. Embassy personnel deal with matters of government policy and serve as their government's eyes, ears, and voice in another country.

The role of a consul is to deal with matters of concern to individual citizens, matters of business or of personal relations in a foreign country. While embassies ordinarily are located in the other country's capital, consulates can be located anywhere in the country.

These offices have officers at three levels: Consuls General, Consuls, and Vice Consuls. Some countries even have Honorary Consuls.

What are the main categories of services that a U.S. embassy or consulate can provide to U.S. citizens abroad?

The two main categories are emergency services and citizens' consular services. A breakdown:

Emergency services in case of:

- Arrest and incarceration.
- Financial destitution.
- Physical or mental illness.
- Death.
- Disappearance.
- Travel advisory needs.
- Search and rescue for ships and planes.

Citizens' consular services in cases of:

- Acquisition and loss of citizenship.
- Passport and registration services abroad.
- International adoptions.
- Consular reports of birth.
- Consular reports of death.

- IRS information and forms.
- Child custody disputes.
- Federal benefits.
- Judicial services.
- Property claims and estates.
- Selective Service registration.
- Shipping and seaman protection.
- Voting.

What are the limits to consular services?

There are both legal and practical limitations.

Legal limitations include both those imposed by federal or state laws of the USA and those imposed by the laws of the host country.

A particular example is the Privacy Act, which limits the right of the consular officer to reveal information about individuals to anyone (including family members and congressional representatives) without the permission of the individual concerned.

Practical limitations include the availability of staff, the availability of local professional help when needed, and the availability of funds from official sources.

Is there any kind of financial assistance that a U.S. embassy or consulate can offer to U.S. citizens abroad?

Yes, but it is extremely limited.

The office will assist in trying to locate private funds from an individual's family or friends in the USA if the individual is destitute or ill and needs help or repatriation.

If that fails, there are two other possibilities.

If no private resources are available, a repatriation loan might be approved to pay for return to the nearest U.S. port of entry. There, the U.S. Department of Health and Human Services takes over and arranges for further assistance in the USA.

In cases of temporary destitution, the consular office might provide a small government loan until private funds arrive.

In all cases, the local consular office, in cooperation with the Emergency Center in Washington, D.C., will help to expedite the arrival of private funds. Contact:

- Citizens Emergency Center
  Department of State
  Washington, DC 20520
  (202) 647-5225

If I am arrested, can a consular officer get me out of jail?

No. Nor can he or she serve as your legal representative. However, consular officers can look out for your welfare in the following ways:

Visit you, usually within 24 hours.

Offer you a list of attorneys and advise you about the local legal system.

Periodically check on your welfare and the observance of your human rights, and report to family and friends.

Deliver private funds.

Arrange needed dietary or medical assistance.

How can the consular officer help if I or a member of my family should die abroad?

The consular officer will assist in the arrangements for returning the remains to the USA or for local burial, as the surviving family desires. There are, however, no grants or loans available.

A consular officer will also provide a "Report of Death of an American Citizen" (Optional Form 180, formerly FS-192), which is an official notice of death.

Finally, the consular officer has statutory responsibility for taking charge of the personal estate of the deceased if there is no legal or personal representative in the country of death. He or she does not, however, take custody of real property.

In what instances would the local U.S. embassy or consulate help to locate U.S. citizens abroad?

There are three situations in which a variety of techniques are used to locate and contact U.S. citizens abroad:

When the U.S. citizen abroad has been out of contact for a long enough period to be presumed missing.

When the U.S. citizen abroad is presumed safe and well but must be located because of a personal or family crisis at home.

When there has been a disaster abroad and U.S. citizens are involved, so that their families can be notified of their situation.

What is the value of Department of State travel advisories?

Travel advisories are issued to alert U.S. citizens overseas to potential problems that may adversely affect their travel. Travel advisories often concern international conflict, civil unrest within individual countries, natural disasters, or outbreaks of disease. Many of the advisories refer to temporary conditions and are canceled when the problem no longer poses a threat to travelers. The advisories are available from U.S. embassies or consulates overseas or in the United States from the Citizens Emergency Center at (202) 647-5225.

Is it useful to register with the nearest U.S. embassy or consulate?

Yes. The information you provide might help the consular officer locate you in case of emergency or when you are traveling in disturbed areas.

What is the local consulate's role in questions of citizenship?

In appropriate cases, the officer can issue a consular report of birth, a U.S. passport, or a card of identity and registration of U.S. citizenship, and can officially record U.S. citizenship at the consular office. This is done at the discretion of the officer on the basis of guidelines and directives issued by the Department of State.

This initial determination is subject to review at higher levels in the Department of State, and persons receiving adverse decisions may be entitled to an administrative hearing and review in the federal courts. When the applicant is in the United States, the Immigration and Naturalization Service is responsible for determination of acquisition of citizenship.

More information on this topic is in Chapter 3, "Citizenship and Nationality."

What is the consular officer's role regarding federal benefits?

In most countries, the monthly benefit checks are mailed or pouched to the U.S. embassy and then distributed through the local postal service. Consular officers, except in the Philippines, assist in the processing of individual benefit claims, investigate claims on behalf of the agency concerned, and perform other tasks as requested or needed by the beneficiary or survivor. Benefits programs include Social Security (retirement, survivors, and disability) checks, veterans' pension checks, railroad retirement checks, and Civil Service retirement pension checks. If you have a problem with your check or your beneficiary status, the consular officer will assist you in reaching the responsible agency.

Some of the services provided sound like legal services, and yet consular officers do not act as attorneys or legal representatives. What are these services and what are the limits?

The service areas are:

- Judicial services.
- Child custody services.
- Estate and property claims services.

However, owing to the limits of consular authority, it is sometimes necessary to use the services of an attorney.

What are included in judicial services?

- Lists of attorneys abroad for use by U.S. citizens.
- Assistance in service of process abroad.
- Transmission of letters rogatory and other evidence-gathering assistance.
- Consular notarial and authentication functions.
- Advice in obtaining foreign public documents.
- Advice on local law and regulations governing marriage.

What function does the consulate serve in child custody disputes?

The function is restricted to:

- Locating children abroad.
- Monitoring their welfare at the request of either parent.
- Providing general information about local laws on child custody and procedures for getting the child back to the USA.
- Providing lists of attorneys abroad who can help a parent.

However, no U.S. consular officer can take custody of a child or influence foreign custody proceedings. Consular officers must respect the laws in the country where the child is located and generally recognize the jurisdiction of local courts.

Can child support orders be enforced abroad with the assistance of consular officials?

The role of the official is to provide advice and to refer the person seeking support to a list of attorneys. Normally, the enforcement proceeding must be conducted through a court in the foreign country.

What are the estate functions if a U.S. citizen dies abroad?

The U.S. consular officer has statutory responsibility for protecting the personal estate of the deceased if there is no legal representative of the person in the country where he or she dies.

This includes:

- Taking physical possession of all personal property (but not real property), including documents and papers.
- Giving receipts to anyone who turns over such items.
- Making an inventory.
- Obtaining appraisals at local value.
- Paying local debts out of available funds.
- Releasing effects according to instructions or otherwise exercising appropriate discretion.

However, any shipping of effects must be by private carrier, although legal documents and correspondence can be sent by diplomatic pouch.

Is help available in settling the estate abroad?

Yes. The consular officer provides guidance in procedures to be followed in preparing letters testamentary, letters of administration, and affidavits of next of kin for establishing legal claims to estates.

What is the property claim function?

Consular officers are allowed to assist in locating and recovering lost, stolen, and confiscated property. They also can help locate lost shipments of goods and might be able to help redress claims for damaged or lesser quality goods shipped from abroad. However, they must stay within the limits of local laws, and their help must be permitted by the local government and Department of State regulations.

Ordinarily, they give general information and make referrals to local attorneys who can be helpful.

Where is more information about consular services available?

For more information about consular services, ask for the consular publication *Tips for Americans Resident Abroad.* Write:

- Bureau of Consular Affairs
  Public Affairs Staff
  CA/PA Room 5807
  Department of State
  Washington, DC 20520

If an emergency arises, is there a number I can call for immediate help?
Yes. The Bureau of Consular Affairs operates the Citizens Emergency Center in Washington, D.C. Call:

- Citizens Emergency Center
  (202) 647-5225
  The phones are staffed on the following schedule:
  8:15 a.m.–10 p.m. EST Monday–Friday
  9 a.m.–3 p.m. EST Saturday

For emergencies on holidays, nights, and weekends, call the above number and a recording will direct you to the appropriate duty officer.

Chapter 8

Voting Abroad

Introduction

Every effort is being made at the federal level to encourage and facilitate voting in U.S. elections by U.S. citizens abroad. The problem is that all elections, including federal elections, are administered at the local government level, usually by county supervisors acting under state and local laws and regulations.

About 6,400 local election jurisdictions are involved in the process, and there is little uniformity.

U.S. citizens abroad vote by absentee ballot. Their rights are governed by federal law:

The Uniformed and Overseas Citizens Absentee Voting Act of 1986 amended and simplified voting procedures. It allows a blank federal absentee ballot to be used in all federal elections.

Any U.S. citizen abroad who wants to vote should remember to register.

Should I register before I go abroad?

Yes, if possible. This will clearly establish your voting residence in the USA, but it will not assure you of receiving an absentee ballot for any upcoming election.

Can I register from abroad?

Yes. You can use Federal Postcard Form 76 to register or to request state registration forms that are required. Most states now accept the postcard as a simultaneous registration and absentee ballot application.

Where can I get the Postcard Form 76?

It should be available from any U.S. military installation or any U.S. embassy or consulate near you. Contact the voting assistance officer or counselor. As a last resort, write to:

- Federal Voting Assistance Program
  Office of the Secretary of Defense
  Pentagon Room 1B457
  Washington, DC 20301

Does it matter that I have no connection with the military or civilian parts of the U.S. government?

No, it doesn't matter. These installations are authorized to assist any and all U.S. citizens.

To whom do I address the postcard?

The postcard form should be addressed to the voting registrar who has jurisdiction over your voting residence.

What is my voting residence?

Your voting residence is your legal residence or domicile in the USA, where you would vote if you were present.

Where can I get the address of the voting registrar at my voting residence?

You can find the addresses of voting registrars in every state and county in the *Voting Assistance Guide* published by the Federal Voting Assistance Program. This book should be available for reference at the nearest military or civilian installation that has a voting assistance officer or counselor.

What if I don't have a legal residence or domicile in the USA or cannot honestly determine where it is?

Federal law provides that in such cases you can vote in the state in which you resided immediately before you left the USA, no matter how long ago and no matter what your intentions are about returning there.

Does this mean that I can vote there in federal and local elections?

You are qualified to vote in federal elections, but not necessarily in local elections. Some states permit both and will send you ballots for both. Other states will send you only a federal ballot.

How can I apply for an absentee ballot from abroad?

Fill out and submit a Federal Postcard Registration and Absentee Ballot Request (Standard Postcard Form 76). There is a separate instruction sheet that is also available and can be useful. You will need to know in what district you last voted.

Should I do this even though I have already registered and requested an absentee ballot by other means?

Yes. When in doubt, file the card again. Do it as soon as you know of an upcoming election.

Is there a single source of information about state laws governing absentee voting?

Yes. The *Voting Assistance Guide* gives a general overview of every state law. This book is revised every election year to reflect changes in state electoral codes.

How do I find out when the primary and general elections are taking place and what offices are being contested?

A table of information is also issued for each biennial general election by the Federal Voting Assistance Program and should be available wherever its material is available.

Where do I find out who is running and the platforms?

You might address requests for information about candidates to the local political party office in the county where you will vote or to the League of Women Voters in Washington, D.C. The voter registrars might be willing to forward your request, but don't count on it.

Do the U.S. political parties have organizations abroad?

Yes. The major parties have organizations abroad. Write:

- Democrats Abroad
  c/o Democratic National Committee
  20 Ivy St. S.E.
  Washington, DC 20003

- Republicans Abroad
  c/o Republican National Committee
  310 First St. S.E.
  Washington, DC 20003

How do party organizations abroad participate in the U.S. political process?

The Democratic Party has had a Democrats Abroad delegation voting at party conventions since 1976. Republicans Abroad had an observer non-voting delegation at the 1984 party convention and hopes to have a voting delegation in 1992. Both groups have had a voice on their respective platform committees.

Who elects the delegates who represent party organizations abroad at the conventions?

Both major parties run political primaries abroad to elect delegates. Any U.S. citizen abroad of voting age can request a ballot from the party of his or her choice in order to vote for delegates.

Can I vote in the political primary abroad and in the U.S. primary also?

No. You must choose whether you wish to vote in the political primary abroad (for president only) or the primary in the USA. In the general election you can vote only in the USA.

Is there any advantage to voting in the political primary abroad for president?

The political primaries abroad for president are designed to give U.S. citizens abroad as a group a voice in the selection of major presidential and vice presidential candidates. Persons who identify more closely with the U.S. community abroad and who want it to have an effective voice should seriously consider the value of participation in the primaries abroad.

American Citizens Abroad believes that U.S. citizens abroad will benefit greatly from identifiable participation in partisan politics, regardless of which party.

What is the most serious obstacle to voting abroad?

Aside from the general complexity of the rules, timing is the major problem. It is easy to send out your postcard early enough (but not too early). But local practices or regulations about when absentee ballots are mailed could prevent your ballot from arriving soon enough to be returned in time for counting.

Even if you mail it back the instant you receive it, the

ballot might arrive too late to be counted. Many states are trying to help by extending ballot transmission time. No matter how late you get your ballot, be sure to vote and return it—it might still be counted, and it will serve to keep you on the electoral rolls.

Is there any long-term solution to the timing problem?

The Uniformed and Overseas Citizens Absentee Voting Act of 1986 created a standard blank absentee ballot to be used in federal elections by voters abroad who have not received a regular absentee ballot in time to return it and have it counted in the election. These ballots can be used only by voters abroad who already have requested a ballot from the state in which they are registered. This ballot is available at military installations and at U.S. embassies and consulates.

If I vote by absentee ballot in a state back home, will I become subject to state taxes of any kind?

Not as long as voting is confined to federal elections. Federal law prohibits the states from considering that in determining whether a person is subject to state or local taxes. However, if you vote in a state election or if you have some other connection with the state, you might be subject to state taxes. The *Voting Assistance Guide* has details about state taxes on foreign-earned income.

Chapter 9

Customs Requirements

Introduction

Clearing customs can add to the hassle of moving from one home to another, one country to another.

Your personal possessions, your household goods, and any gifts you carry are all subject to inspection. It is impossible to cover all the rules that apply to these situations. They are complex and change frequently. But a few important points can help you get started.

Will I have to pay customs duty on the things I ship to my new home abroad?

Possibly. You should check this in advance to minimize the possibility of any expense. An experienced mover can be helpful. A letter from your employer stating your business "to whom it may concern" might be useful.

Are there any restrictions on what I can take abroad?

Only articles that are illegal to have in your possession in the first place are illegal to take out of the USA. But the country of your destination might have restrictions, so it is best to check on any unusual items you want to take with you.

Are there restrictions on what I can bring back to the USA when I return?

Yes, and they are numerous. You should check very carefully with the U.S. Customs Service and obtain their current literature before trying to bring back exotic or unusual items.

What about my ordinary household effects and personal possessions?

Generally, they are not subject to customs duty if you have had such items for a year or more for personal use and if you are a returning resident who went abroad to travel, work, or study. Be certain to retain date-of-purchase receipts.

How can I be certain that the things I take abroad will not be questioned when I return, especially those things that were made abroad but purchased in the USA?

Your best bet is to maintain a proof of prior possession. If you do not have bills of sale or registration numbers or certificates, insurance policies (even lapsed ones) listing specific items and appraisals made in the USA might be accepted.

It is helpful to have an inventory made of everything you take with you. Attach it to your shipping manifest or insurance. Then retain this as a record.

What about my pets?

Your pets will need proof of up-to-date inoculations. They also will need containers acceptable to the shipper and proper documentation for shipping and disembarkation. Certain birds and animals are prohibited. To take pets abroad, it is wise to obtain current information from a U.S. consulate or the customs officer at an embassy.

How can I get information and answers to any questions I have about customs duties?

The U.S. Customs Service publication, *Know Before You Go*, lists rules, as well as addresses and phone numbers for detailed information. Ask for it and any other current booklets. Write:

- U.S. Customs Service
  Washington, DC 20229

Chapter 10

Writing Congress

Introduction

People who live abroad for years, with only brief home leaves, sometimes feel that their opinions and questions on issues do not count with their congressmen and congresswomen. But they do count! What you need to do to be remembered and counted is: Stay in touch!

Rep. Morris K. Udall, D-Ariz., explains the importance of constituent mail to congressmen and congresswomen and how to be more effective in using this vital communication.

The Right to Write

By Hon. Morris K. Udall

Surprisingly few people ever write their congressman. Perhaps 90 percent of our citizens live and die without ever taking pen in hand and expressing a single opinion to the person who represents them in Congress—a person whose vote might decide what price they will pay for acts of government, either in dollars or in human lives.

Mail to a modern-day congressman is more important than ever before. In the days of Calhoun, Clay, Webster and Lincoln, congressmen lived among their people for perhaps nine months of the year. Through daily contacts in a constituency of less than 50,000 people (I represent 10 times that many) they could feel rather completely informed on their constituents' beliefs and feelings.

Today, with the staggering problems of government and increasingly long sessions I must not only vote on many more issues than early-day congressmen but I rarely get to spend more than 60 days a year in Arizona. Thus my mailbag is my best hotline to the people back home.

Some suggestions that apply to all congressional mail:

Address it properly.

- Hon. __________
  U.S. House of Representatives
  Washington, DC 20515
  Or
- Hon. __________
  U.S. Senate
  Washington, DC 20510

Identify the bill or issue. About 20,000 bills are introduced into each Congress, so it is important to be specific. If you write about a bill, try to give the bill number or describe it by a popular title, such as "truth in lending" or "minimum wage."

The letter should be timely. Sometimes a bill is out of committee or has passed the House before a helpful letter arrives. Inform your congressman while there is still time to take action.

Concentrate on your own delegation. All letters written by

residents of my district to other congressmen will be referred to me for reply, and vice versa.

Be reasonably brief. Every working day the mailman leaves 150 or more pieces of mail at my office. For example, it is not necessary that letters be typed—only that they be legible—and the form, phraseology, and grammar are completely unimportant.

Student letters are welcome. Their opinions are important.

Write your own views—not someone else's. A personal letter is far better than a form letter or signature on a petition. For example, I usually know what the major lobbying groups are saying, but I don't often know of your experiences and observations, or what the proposed bill will do to—and for—you.

Give your reasons for taking a stand. For example, I might not know all the effects of the bill and what it might mean to an important segment of my constituency.

Be constructive. If a bill deals with a problem you admit exists, but you believe the bill is the wrong approach, tell what the right approach is.

If you have an expert knowledge, share it with your congressman. For example, I can't possibly be an expert in all fields, but many of my constituents are experts in some of them. I welcome their advice and counsel.

Say "well done" when it is deserved. Congressional representatives are human, too, and they appreciate an occasional "well done" from people who believe they have done the right thing. I know I do. But even if you think I went wrong on an issue, I would welcome a letter telling me you disagreed; it might help me on another issue later.

Some Don'ts:

Don't make threats or promises.

Don't berate your congressman.

Don't pretend to wield vast political influence.

Don't try to instruct your congressman on every issue that comes up. Don't be a pen pal.

In conclusion: During the two-year life of this Congress, the House clerk will record my votes on more than 250 issues. But in a very real sense these will not be my votes, they will be yours, too.

Chapter 11

Services for U.S. Citizens Abroad

Citizens of the USA living abroad often need unusual services because of their unusual situations.

To meet this demand, several companies that cater to the international community have been formed to help U.S. citizens living and traveling abroad.

American Citizens Abroad lists these companies solely as a reference. ACA is not affiliated with any of these companies.

IRC Worldwide Ltd.

IRC has, since 1974, initiated and developed a worldwide network of offices and counselors providing a wide range of services for companies relocating families internationally. Employees can ease into the foreign location without the tensions and frustrations usually associated with a move abroad, supported by bilingual counselors well versed in local customs and property practice. Staff assigned abroad are guided through the transfer process efficiently and sympathetically within company policy guidelines.

- Corporate Headquarters:
  Premier House, 10 Greycoat Place
  London SWIP 1SB
  Tel: 01-222 8866 Fax: 01-799 1521
  Telex: 299078 IRCLON

- New York Office:
  140 Riverside Drive
  New York, NY 10024
  (212) 496-2617

Organization Resources Counselors Inc.

Organization Resources Counselors Inc. is a consulting firm offering professional assistance to management in dealing with the human resources of organizations.

The firm provides needed data for constructive expatriate pay packages. Such data include goods and services (cost-of-living) differentials, foreign and home country housing costs, rates of exchange, and hardship allowances. It also publishes two journals on compensation-related issues and conducts annual surveys of international personnel practices and compensation. Its consulting services include expatriate policy development, communications programs, in-house staff training, and streamlining expatriate administration.

For more information, contact:

- Organization Resources Counselors Inc.
  1211 Avenue of the Americas
  New York, NY 10036
  (212) 790-9204

Control Risks Limited

Control Risks Limited is an international security consulting firm with offices in Bethesda, Md., London, England, Melbourne, Australia, and The Hague, Netherlands. The company offers both hard copy and on-line information subscription services evaluating threats to personnel and assets resulting from political instability, terrorism, and crime. Travel Security Guide, an on-line system, offers detailed advice on more than 70 countries to the international traveler.

Control Risks also prepares contingency plans covering emergency evacuation, kidnap, or extortion. It gives security advice on improving the safety of personnel living or traveling abroad, covering residences, offices, factories, leisure activities, and travel.

The company draws on both its U.S. and international resources to provide extensive advice to U.S. citizens living and traveling abroad.

For more information, contact:

- Executive Director
  Control Risks Limited
  4350 East-West Highway
  Suite 900
  Bethesda, MD 20814
  (301) 654-2075

International Orientation Resources

International Orientation Resources is a consulting firm that provides support services to corporate personnel transferring internationally. Group and individual programs include:

- Screening and selection for assignments abroad.
- Cross-cultural training and orientation.
- Dual Career Workshop for Overseas Transferees.
- Briefing for management and business travelers.
- Logistics support upon arrival in 24 cities worldwide.
- Repatriation workshops.
- Foreign family orientation to the USA.
- English as a second language and foreign language training.
- Communication effectiveness for foreign managers.

For more information, contact:

- Director of Marketing
  International Orientation Resources
  707 Skokie Blvd., Suite 350
  Northbrook, IL 60062
  (312) 205-0066

Going International

Going International is a series of films, videotapes, and training guides produced by Copeland Griggs Productions to prepare the business traveler and the overseas resident for international business, living, and travel.

The series includes:

Bridging the Culture Gap. Illustrates how fundamental cultural differences affect the way business is done abroad.

Managing the Overseas Assignment. Shows specific problems of U.S. citizens who do business abroad. Describes strategies for improving performance.

Beyond Culture Shock. Explains the psychological phases of adjustment. Gives particular attention to spouses' and children's needs in relocation.

Welcome Home, Stranger. Focuses on the unexpected problems of returning home.

Going International: How to Make Friends and Deal Effectively in the Global Marketplace. An in-depth guide to negotiating, marketing, managing people, training, communicating, and managing personal life abroad. Available in hardback and paperback.

For more information, contact:

- Copeland Griggs Productions
  302 23rd Avenue
  San Francisco, CA 94121
  (415) 668-4200
  Fax: (415) 668-6004

Alexander & Alexander Inc.

Alexander & Alexander Inc. is a worldwide insurance brokerage, risk management, and consulting firm with more than 180 offices in 70 countries. The Washington, D.C., office specializes in international relocation insurance services.

Its programs center around a comprehensive international transit insurance package designed to insure household goods, personal effects, and private passenger automobiles while in the course of transit to and from anywhere in the world. In addition, it offers overseas in-residence programs, including coverage for personal liability and storage damage. Comprehensive claims adjusting and settling services are also provided.

For more information, contact:

- Alexander & Alexander Inc.
  2001 L St. N.W.
  Washington, DC 20036
  (202) 296-6440
  Fax: (202) 887-0173
  Telex: 892527 ALEX ALEX WSH

Immunization Alert

Immunization Alert is an international health database providing information on health risks in more than 200 countries. These services are available to individual travelers and corporations.

For more information, contact:

- Medical Director
  Immunization Alert
  P.O. Box 406
  Storrs, CT 06268
  (203) 487-0422
  Telex: 650-290-7868

International SOS Assistance Inc.

International SOS Assistance Inc. offers medical and personal services to corporations and individual members worldwide. Physicians, nurses, and other specialists comprise an international network that is on duty 24 hours a day, 7 days a week, to receive client telephone calls.

SOS provides an extensive range of services in the case of serious injury or illness of a member, including medical supervision, evacuation, access to interpreters, legal assistance, and family care.

For more information, contact:

- International SOS Assistance Inc.
  P.O. Box 11568
  Philadelphia, PA 19116
  (215) 244-1500 or
  (800) 523-8930

International Legal Defense Counsel

International Legal Defense Counsel (ILDC) provides legal assistance to U.S. citizens in foreign countries in civil and criminal law matters, including arrest, imprisonment, divorce, child custody, real estate, wills and estates, etc. Their services include:

Legal counseling. ILDC hires attorneys in foreign countries, coordinates legal representation, and acts as a liaison between the client and the foreign attorney, the family, the corporation, the employee assistance programs, and the U.S. government in civil and criminal cases.

Legal opinions. ILDC provides written legal opinions and analyses on a wide range of matters involving the civil or criminal laws of the host country.

Legal orientation. ILDC provides individual, family, and corporate orientation to the laws and legal customs of any country.

For more information, contact:

- International Legal Defense Counsel
  24th Floor, Packard Building
  111 S. 15th St.
  Philadelphia, PA 19102
  (215) 977-9982
  Fax: 215 564 2859
  Telex: 215 493 0187 ILDCUI

Moran, Stahl & Boyer Inc.

The international division of Moran, Stahl & Boyer Inc. is a consulting firm providing training in foreign business practices, a training and assessment service for foreign assignments, foreign language instruction, and re-entry programs for the returning international executive.

For more information, contact:

- Moran, Stahl & Boyer Inc.
  900 28th Street
  Boulder, CO 80303
  (303) 449-8440

Book Distributors

The following companies are experienced in finding books for U.S. citizens living abroad:

The Flying Book

In addition to finding books for U.S. citizens abroad, The Flying Book will wrap and mail books as gifts from you to others.

Most books can usually be sent within a week. Checks drawn on U.S. banks are accepted. Credit cards are not.

For more information:

- Mary Knapp
  The Flying Book
  P.O. Box 465
  South Egremont, MA 01258
  (413) 528-1055

The Wine and Food Library

As the name suggests, cookbooks and books on wine are the specialty here. The oldest volume dates to 1502. U.S. checks or money orders are accepted. No credit cards. Catalogs are available. Price: $2 for the regular catalog, $5 for the rare-item catalog.

For more information:

- Jan Longone
  The Wine and Food Library
  1207 West Madison St.
  Ann Arbor, MI 48103
  (313) 663-4894

Book Call

Book Call ships all kinds of books worldwide and will track down hard-to-get volumes. Specialty: business and economics-related titles. Customers receive regular newsletters. Accepts checks and money orders in U.S. funds. Also takes American Express, Visa, and MasterCard.

For more information:

- Faye DeWitt
  Book Call
  59 Elm Street
  New Canaan, CT 06840
  (203) 966-5470

Wayfarer Books

Travel and outdoor books are the specialty at Wayfarer. They send out a travel catalog and a catalog of new books from university presses. Checks drawn on U.S. banks accepted.

For more information:

- Tom and Judy Betts
  Wayfarer Books
  P.O. Box 1121
  Davenport, IA 52805
  (319) 355-3902